150th Logo Designs: Roberta Avidor and Kelly Newcomer

Design and production: Mikki Morrissette, Be-Mondo Publishing Inc.

Design consultant: Mary Leir, Leir Design

Images are from the archives of First Universalist Church of Minneapolis, including the collection housed at the Minnesota History Center, and the following photographers: Mike Casserly, Tom Jackson, Janet Mills, Sharon Ramirez, Dale Schwie and Jessica Wicks. Thanks to Minnesota Orchestra for picture of Emil Oberhoffer.

Editing: Mikki Morrissette and Kathy Coskran

Timeline written by John Addington

Church building illustrations by Fran Addington

Introductory sections written by: Kathy Coskran

Appendix and Index compiled by: Nancy Atchison, Carol Jackson, Mary Junge, Marcia Wattson, Karin Wille

Printing: Bookmobile, St. Louis Park, Minnesota

For further information about the Sesquicentennial events, articles and more, see

FirstUniv150.org

Copyright © 2009 by First Universalist Church of Minneapolis. All rights reserved.

For inquiries or additional copies, please contact First Universalist Church at:
3400 Dupont Avenue South
Minneapolis, MN 55408

First printing, October 2009

ISBN: 978-0-9772042-4-3

First Universalist Church of Minneapolis:

The First 150 Years

This book is the culmination of the work of many devoted archivists, and is dedicated to them with gratitude and admiration by the Sesquicentennial Steering Committee.

Special appreciation goes to John Addington, church historian for many years, who generously gave many hours of his time, his talent and his passion for history to this enterprise.

(August 9, 1926 — September 25, 2009)

"*Only that day dawns to which we are awake.*"
— John Addington's favorite quote, from Henry David Thoreau's *Walden*

First Universalist Church of Minneapolis: The First 150 Years

The Beginnings: 1859-1939 1
- Early Days 3
- Lakewood Cemetery 7
- Minnesota Orchestra Roots 9
- Ministers 11
- Members 17
- Women's Organizations 21
- Unity House 23
- Church Homes 28

Moving Forward: 1939-2009 33
- The Times 35
- Ministers and Staff 37
- Members 52
- Church Homes 56

This We Believe 61
- The Faith Tradition 63
- Congregational Life 69
- Rites of Passage 70
- Faith Development 75
- Music: A Song is Rising 79
- The Arts: Beauty Before Us 82
- Congregational Polity 85
- Words from the Pulpit 89
- Statements from Members 108

By Our Deeds 109
- An Act of Love: Caring for Each Other 111
- The Association of Universalist Women 113
- A Welcoming Congregation 118
- First Universalist Foundation 121
- Unity Summer 123
- Working for Peace Since World War II 126

Illuminate the Past, Celebrate the Present, Inspire the Future 133
- Illuminate the Past 135
- Celebrate the Present 139
- Inspire the Future 141
- The Reverend Justin Schroeder 143
- We Will: In Words and Pictures 145
- Dreams and Legacies 150

Acknowledgements 151

Appendix 153

Index 160

Charles Darwin published *On the Origin of Species.* About 2,600 people called Minneapolis home, one year after Minnesota became a state. A few of them were Universalists.

They gathered on October 24 at the Cataract House hotel, at what is now the intersection of Washington and Portland Avenues, to form the First Universalist Society.

The first church, a wooden structure at Fifth Street and Fourth Avenue South, was completed. It seated 400 and contained the city's first pipe organ. It was known to local jokesters as "the church with cushions in the pews and no hell."

Keyes, in ill health, resigned and was replaced by the Reverend James Tuttle.

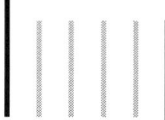

1859   1866   1875

1864   1876

The congregation, meeting in rented quarters, called the Reverend Joseph W. Keyes as its first settled minister.

The city and the church had grown dramatically. The outgrown wooden building was replaced by a stone church at Eighth Street and Second Avenue South with seating for more than 1,000 worshipers. Tuttle chose the name Church of the Redeemer for the congregation, although it legally remained First Universalist Society.

The church was badly damaged by fire on a very cold January Sunday. It was enlarged and rebuilt immediately.

Shutter died in office at the age of 87. The church had grown old and infirm along with him, and was close to death itself. There were 30 to 40 worshipers in that huge sanctuary on a Sunday. The Reverend Carl Olson succeeded Shutter.

1888   1900   1925   1939

1891

Tuttle retired after a 25-year-ministry that set a trend: four senior ministers in 120 years. He was succceded by the Reverend Marion D. Shutter, associate minister since 1886.

With the war over and church membership growing under Olson's leadership, a Jeffersonian-style building was completed at 50th Street and Girard Avenue South.

1950

1975

1941

The Catholic Archdiocese bought the church building. The congregation intended to build a church in south Minneapolis, but Pearl Harbor intervened. World War II meant no building materials for civilian use, so the congregation moved into a house at 4600 Dupont Avenue South. It became known as Church House, with meeting space downstairs and school rooms upstairs.

1963

Carl Olson resigned because of ill health. The Reverend John Cummins came out from Massachusetts to succeed him.

The need for a bigger structure had become pressing. The church was overcrowded, with no way to expand the 230-seat building. The answer was the purchase of the Adath Jeshurun Synagogue at 3400 Dupont Avenue South. It offered seating for 900, plus much more church school space.

The Reverend Frank Rivas was called as senior minister, and the Reverend Kate Tucker was soon called as associate.

Cummins retired.

Rivas resigned.

1986   1993   1997   2000   2007

1988   1995   2009

Sweetser and Milnor resigned.

After a two-year interim period, the husband-and-wife co-ministry of Terry Sweetser and Susan Milnor began, and with it a surge in membership.

The Reverend Justin Schroeder was called as senior minister.

PREFACE

When the Sesquicentennial Communications Committee began meeting in Fall 2007, the intention was to illuminate the past history of First Universalist Church of Minneapolis in writing. We were inspired from the beginning by the words of the Reverend Marion D. Shutter, who said in his address at the church's 50th anniversary celebration: *"The great questions by which any church must be judged are: What have its ideas and its people done for the community? What kind of men and women has it produced? What has been the character of their deeds?"*

In exploring the answers to these questions, the committee identified themes and topics for research and recruited volunteers to research and write the articles. The purpose was to discover and disseminate who our forebears were and what were their contributions to the city of Minneapolis. What are the threads that connect us to the past in the areas of civic engagement, peace and justice, human rights and theology? Who were we and who are we as a unique religious community?

We decided to publish inserts in the Liberal newsletter highlighting key individuals and actions that reflected and shaped our values. We wanted to make this information as widely available as possible, so the FirstUniv150.org website was developed as an archive.

Though we had not originally planned to publish a history of our congregation's first 150 years as a book, we did think it a good idea to print a compilation of the Liberal articles. The end result is so much more than we had imagined. There are new photographs, sermon excerpts, articles, and additional information in sidebars and quotes.

This book is a natural outgrowth of the enthusiasm generated by team research. The writers developed a palpable fondness for the characters in our church's history, almost as if they came to know them personally. We wanted to share and preserve the stories and characters. Writers are credited in the Acknowledgements on page 151.

Phil Burke offered to research and compile a list of names of members from the past 150 years. He was inspired to take on this task by remembering the powerful impact of seeing the names on the Vietnam War Memorial in Washington, D.C. Thanks to those efforts, this is now a list of 5,562 people (and growing) who have made the pledge of membership.

Those who have dug in to do this exploration have gained insights and inspiration that is both gratifying and inspiring. We hope that some part of that inspiration will be shared by others who take the journey started here.

—Marcia Wattson, Chair, Sesquicentennial Communications Committee
The committee consisted of John Addington, Phil Burke, Mary Junge,
Peg Meier, Mikki Morrissette and Craig Wilkins

Introduction

History is who we are and why we are the way we are. — David McCullough

This book is the history of the First Universalist Church of Minneapolis—the story of **who we are**. We are a church founded by people who brought their brand of liberal Christianity to the frontier town that was Minneapolis in 1859. We are a congregation whose members helped found many of Minneapolis' institutions, from Lakewood Cemetery to the park system to General Mills to the Minneapolis Public Library. We are a church whose ministers debated both sides of the evolution question, founded the first settlement house in Minneapolis and marched with Dr. Martin Luther King, Jr. We are a congregation that went from being a downtown church in the 1880s with a sanctuary that held 1,000 people, to a congregation of 40 that met in a house during the 1940s, to a congregation that in the late 1990s moved to a church with a sanctuary that held 900. We are a congregation that believed in "one God, whose nature is Love," in "the supreme worth of every personality," and that "love is the doctrine of this church."

This book is also the story of **why we are the way we are**. The First Universalist Foundation exists today because of the legacy of Unity House. Our name traces its lineage to the First Universalist Society and the Church of the Redeemer, the names our congregation used for its first 100 years. Unity Summer and the Youth Cultural Exchange have their roots in the youth programs of Unity House. Our child dedication ritual of today evolved from a christening of yesteryear. The voting rights and reproductive choice work of the Association of Universalist Women in the twenty-first century had its genesis in the social reform work of the Women's Association of the twentieth century. Our congregation's commitment today to "justice, equity and compassion in human relationships" flows directly from our congregation's earlier commitment to "overcome evil and progressively establish the kingdom of God" here on earth.

This book is the story of **who we are and why we are the way we are**. It is a story of a people who committed from their beginnings 150 years ago to help one another and to work together to serve the twin causes of religion and truth. It is a story of a people who believed in the universal saving power of a God of love and who believe today in the saving power of the Universalist message of love and hope. It is the story of the people of First Universalist Church. May we know this story and honor it in our words and deeds, for today and for times we shall never see.

—Karin Wille, Co-Chair, Sesquicentennial Steering Committee
October 2009

THE BEGINNINGS: 1859-1939

Our church will live as long, and as long only, as its living will be of use in the world. The question of our future is a question of faithfulness and zeal. No opportunity seems greater, no mission wider, no prospect brighter than ours.

—the Reverend James Tuttle, 1889,
at the dedication of the
Church of the Redeemer (left)
rebuilt after a devastating fire a year earlier

THE BEGINNINGS: 1859-1939

The Cataract House was the first home of the congregation we are today.

On October 24, 1859, only 16 years after the first house was built by Europeans in Minneapolis, a small group met at the Cataract House on the corner of what is now Washington and Portland Avenues to create the First Universalist Society of Minneapolis. It was not the first Universalist church to be formed in the new territory, but it was the only one that survived 150 years.

In 1876, the First Universalist Society became known as the Church of the Redeemer when the congregation dedicated its new church building at Eighth Street and Second Avenue. In 1952 it became the First Universalist Church of Minneapolis. When the church celebrated the sesquicentennial on October 24, 2009, First Universalist Church was not only the oldest continuous Unitarian Universalist congregation in Minnesota, but also the largest Universalist church in the United States.

Beginnings matter. The congregation today stands on the shoulders of giants. First Universalist Church of Minneapolis was created by the same men and women who laid the foundation for Minneapolis. The early ministers were household names throughout the city; later ministers were activists. The early members were influential in establishing the Minneapolis library system, establishing the first fire department, founding the Minneapolis public school system, creating the Minneapolis park system, setting aside land for Lakewood Cemetery, founding Unity House and more.

This first section, *The Beginnings*, is a snapshot of the powerful beginnings of First Universalist Church of Minneapolis.

Early Days

What a difference 150 years can make!

When the founders of First Universalist met on October 24, 1859, Minneapolis was a new frontier town in a one-year-old state. Just a year earlier a local newspaper ran a front-page headline in six-inch type: Minnesota is Admitted Into the Union!

Minnesota was officially a state, but in many respects, it was still a wild, untamed place. The men and women who founded that early Universalist church were among the best educated and civic-minded of the early groups to settle west of the Mississippi River and became inextricably connected to the region's growth and development. They came for the rich farmland, for business opportunities and for the climate, always described as promoting health. A state publication bragged, *"The atmosphere in Minnesota in the winter is like wine, so exhilarating in its effects on the system ... The extreme cold does not last but a few days."*

Minutes of the Original Meeting

Pursuant to a notice duly given, the undersigned met at the Cataract House in Minneapolis on Monday Evening the 24th day of October, A. D. 1859.

On motion, W. D. Washburn was called to the chair and Richard Strout was elected Secretary "Pro Tem".

The following preamble and constitution was read and adopted:

"We, the undersigned, being desirous of promoting the cause of liberal christianity in this community hereby unite for that purpose agreeing to be governed by the following constitution."

Article 1st. This Association shall be known as the "First Universalist Society of Minneapolis".

Article 2nd. The officers of this society shall consist of Five Trustees, a Secretary and Treasurer, all of whom shall be elected annually by ballot at the regular annual meeting.

Article 3rd. Any person may become a member of this society by a vote of a majority of the members present at any regular meeting and who shall have made written application for membership to the Trustees.

Article 4th. The annual meeting of the society shall be held on the 1st Monday of October and regular meetings of the Society shall be held on the 1st Monday of each month.

Article 5th. This Constitution may be altered or amended by a vote of two-thirds of the members present at any regular meeting, providing such alteration or amendment shall have been proposed in a regular meeting at least one month previous to action being taken upon it.

The following officers were then elected by ballot:

WM. D. GARLAND   THOMAS H. PERKINS
F. R. E. CORNELL   W. D. WASHBURN
H. J. PLUMER
Trustees

WM. B. CORNELL :: :: :: :: Secretary
GEORGE E. W. CROCKER :: :: :: Treasurer

On motion of W. D. Washburn the Secretary was directed to purchase such books as the Society need for the transcribing of this preamble and constitution and the minutes of all meetings of the Society.

On motion, Society adjourned to first Monday in November next, at the same place at 7 o'clock P. M.

RICHARD STROUT
Secretary "Pro Tem."

The propaganda was convincing. First Universalist's second settled minister, the Reverend James Tuttle and his wife, Harriet, came to Minneapolis in 1866 for her health. As it turned out, her physical well-being did not improve in the "exhilarating" climate, but their ministry had a lasting effect on the growth of Universalism in the new state and in the formation of the city of Minneapolis.

Minnesota Bounty
It was the Mississippi River, and particularly the Falls of St. Anthony,

An active dues-paying member of the women's groups at First Universalist Church, Esther Friedlander (1870-1959) wrote poetry that was often read at the Christmas tea of the Association of Universalist Women. She taught Latin at South High School and is buried at Lakewood Cemetery.

Sea Shells

All day the wind-tossed sea has cast

Upon the sand these lovely forms

Of shell, now tenantless. What storms

Such fragile beauty can outlast!

—Esther Friedlander, *The North America Book of Verse*, Volume 4, 1939

that brought settlement. First came St. Anthony, the town on the east side of the river, and then Minneapolis on the west. The falls were beautiful, but more importantly, necessary as a source of power. In the 1850s, the two small towns grew impressively: in that one decade, their combined population grew by 10 times, and by 1872 Minneapolis absorbed St. Anthony to become the state's largest city.

Most newcomers, including our founders, were from the East. The early Universalists were a fraction of the total population, with the advantage of a strong education from New England colleges. They came from places where stores stocked the everyday necessities. Not so in the new state, where obtaining food was a primary concern.

The merging of the wild and the domestic was a daily occurrence. Charles M. Loring often told about a bear that visited founding member William Drew Washburn's summer garden in 1861, "eating all of his sweet corn, no one having the courage to dispute Bruin's claims." Roving timberwolves made the raising of small domestic animals nearly impossible. Even adult cattle were at risk. Raising chickens was the best way to ensure nightly, or even midday, visits by foxes, which did not yet fear people. Deer were so abundant that it was said any decent marksman could keep the larder stocked with venison. Bear meat and small game—rabbits, squirrel, quail and prairie chickens—also were obtained easily. Fish were plentiful but the nearby lakes soon were depleted because the settlers netted, salted and stored large quantities.

New England of the West

The transplanted Yankees brought the arts to the Twin Cities in the 1850s. Bookstores opened. The University of Minnesota was founded. Newspapers flourished. Churches of many denominations opened including other Universalist churches. Dorilus Morrison, the first mayor of Minneapolis, was one of the early members of the First Universalist Society of Minneapolis and would serve as president of the Board of Trustees for 31 years, until his death in 1897.

In May 1859 the Young Men's Library Association was organized as a subscription library that within a year would incorporate as the Minneapolis Athenaeum. By 1885 an Athenaeum subcommittee would complete work in establishing the Minneapolis Public Library. The new library board consisted almost entirely of Universalists.

The Beginnings: 1859-1939

The Union School, viewed as the foundation of the Minneapolis public school system, opened in 1858 with 320 students. Although Minneapolis and St. Anthony were consolidated in 1872, it took six more years before the two school systems were united. The first school board included Morrison as president and several First Universalist members.

However, the new city struggled to provide basic services. Law enforcement agencies grappled with such common offenses as drunkenness, prostitution, gambling, theft and disorderly conduct. Many municipal needs continued to be challenging, including issues of public health and water supply. Free-ranging cattle were a major source of water contamination. Pools of standing water were everywhere, and outhouses were a common sight as late as 1920.

The first fire companies were organized in St. Anthony in the 1850s. Each member had to equip himself "with two wooden pails for carrying water and a large canvas bag, in which articles rescued from the flames could be deposited." By the fall of 1865 Universalist George A. Brackett proposed "that a rotary pump be installed in the basement of the Cataract Flour Mill to furnish water in case of fire." On January 16, 1868, Mayor Morrison presided over a meeting of 102 people to complete the organization of a fire department and the Minneapolis Hook and Ladder Company No. 1 was born.

As early as 1869 our ever-progressive city passed a resolution in support of a park system. Among those most prominent in urging these matters were Universalists Loring, Brackett and future Congressman William S. King. An 1873 council resolution stated that no plat should be accepted by the city unless a portion of the land included in it be dedicated to park purposes. In 1883 a Minneapolis park commission was established. The first 12 commissioners included 4 Universalists.

Even a frontier city has the poor and the elderly, and members of the First Universalist Society were proactive in seeing that they were provided for. In 1886 William D. Washburn co-founded the Washburn Memorial Orphan Home at 50th Street and Nicollet Avenue South for the care of up to 100 children. The home was endowed by a bequest from his brother, Cadwallader, in honor of their mother. The Washburn

William Drew Washburn, nicknamed Young Rapid by his family
COURTESY OF ANN GAMLIN

Moderator of the first church meeting in 1859 was the young William D. Washburn, who would go on to become a member of the Board of Trustees at First Universalist for 50 years, including serving as president.

One of my earliest recollections is of walking to church . . . the gentle rustle of Mother's stiff silk gown . . . Father's tall silk hat, long Sunday coat and sporty cane.

—*Early Minneapolis Memories,* by Universalist Maud Conkey Stockwell

Home became the Washburn Child Guidance Center, which eventually opened branches in north Minneapolis, Hopkins and Maple Grove.

In 1888, First Universalist Harvey Brown provided $10,500 toward 80 acres of property on Cedar Lake for the establishment of a "Home for Aged Women and a retreat for retired ministers and their wives." The Jones-Harrison Home for Aged Women was the result.

The concept of summer-supervised public playgrounds in Minneapolis was first envisioned by Charles M. Loring, who called a general meeting in 1898 to establish a committee to make recommendations. Universalist committee members included Charles M. Jordan, superintendent of schools, and the Reverend Marion Shutter. Mrs. Loring, Mrs. Shutter and the Mothers' Club of Unity House supported and expanded a program for playgrounds and vacation schools, which eventually became part of the public school system.

A crowning jewel of the early years was Unity House, founded in 1897 to respond to the need in north Minneapolis for a free kindergarten. The house originated at 1616 Washington Avenue North, largely under the direction of Shutter and his wife, Mary, with extensive support from the Church of the Redeemer. As Shutter wrote to the Board of Trustees in 1907, when funds were needed to expand into a new building, the kindergarten had an average attendance of 39, the Mothers' Club had 100 enrolled, and the day nursery served 79 infants, enabling 50 mothers to earn a conservative estimate of $2,500. The sewing school enrolled 130. The library department enrolled 664 children, who drew out 4,455 books that year. There were 70 volunteers who helped at different times of the year. "There is no space to speak of the Summer outings and playgrounds, or of the Unity Camp at Lake Independence last August, which gave 48 working girls and others a breath of country air. Unity House through its various agencies, touches in one way or another from 1,000 to 1,500 children during the year and 600 adults."

The city was young, the church was new, but the two grew together to create a civic landscape that welcomed and cared for a growing population and helped create the institutions that have made Minneapolis the progressive city it is today.

—*Peg Meier with contributions from Dave Juncker and others*

The members of your Church and Society have been more to me than even my own . . . co-workers in everything pertaining to the building up of this city we love so much. So many of your people come from Maine . . . that you might have called them the Pine-Tree Congregation: D. Morrison, W.D. Washburn, Paris Gibson, John Dudley, C.M. Loring, H.F. Brown, W.D. Hale, John Crosby, Fred and Frank Gilson, Rufus Stevens and many others known to you . . . backed up by people of other states: Judge Cornell, Thomas Lowry, Col. King, Judge Koon, W.G. Northrup, George Partridge, W.P. Roberts, E.W. Herrick.

—letter from George A. Brackett in honor of the 50th anniversary celebration

The Beginnings: 1859-1939

LAKEWOOD CEMETERY AND CHAPEL

Lakewood Cemetery was founded in 1871, four years after Minneapolis was incorporated as a city. In July 1871, Colonel William S. King, a local businessman, newspaper publisher, and member of the First Universalist Society, proposed to community leaders of the city that they work together to establish a cemetery in Minneapolis where "the encroachments of the city would never seriously interfere."

It was Dorilus Morrison, the Board of Trustee president from 1859 to 1897 and first mayor of Minneapolis, who called the first meeting to organize a cemetery association. On August 7, 1871, a group of men met to form the Lyndale Cemetery Association. In addition to Morrison and King, other Universalist members at the meeting were William D. Washburn, Thomas Lowry and Charles Loring. At a time when a house in Minneapolis cost $500, the cemetery trustees voted to raise $25,000 to purchase and improve land owned by King located between Lakes Harriet and Calhoun. A.B. Barton became superintendent of the Lyndale Cemetery Association. (The name was later changed to Lakewood.) C.W. Folsom, superintendent of Mount Auburn Cemetery in Cambridge, Massachusetts, developed plans for the grounds.

While the land on which the Lakewood Cemetery rests was not the first choice of the founders, it turned out to be a fitting location. A few blocks from the present building at 34th Street and Dupont Avenue, its gates lead directly to Hennepin Avenue, a major city artery that was once an ancient Dakota trail linking the city lakes with the Mississippi River. At the time of its founding, however, the land was on the south edge of the city, not central at all.

The public dedication was held on September 16, 1872. Women and girls wore their best long skirts or dresses, and their hands, covered in white gloves, gripped their sun parasols. The boys wore their best shirts and pants, and the men wore suits and silk top hats. The ceremony began at 2 p.m. with an address by the Reverend James Tuttle, minister of First Universalist Society, who said: "No ancient necropolis of Babylonia, Egypt, or Rome excelled the Pere-Lachaise of Paris, Mount Auburn of Boston, or Green-Wood of New York; none of the ancient monuments, shady groves, and winding walks seen in those bygone ages

Founders of Lakewood Cemetery included First Universalist members (top to bottom) Colonel William S. King, Charles M. Loring, and Thomas Lowry.

Lakewood interior designer Charles Lamb spoke of religious symbolism when the building was dedicated in 1910: "Religion, if it means anything, is not a hopeless form. Religion means a spiritual uplifting, and if we place faith on one side and hope before us, and follow with love, we add a fourth dimension of memory, because enshrined in your hearts and minds must always be the memory of those we have lost."

were more skillfully and tastefully wrought than those which meet our eye to-day. . . . Our affection for our friends when living is understood most by the care we take of their graves when they have passed away."

The Memorial Chapel at Lakewood is listed on the National Register of Historic Places and serves as the architectural focal point of the cemetery. The building was designed by prominent Minneapolis architect Harry Wild Jones and was modeled after the Hagia Sophia in Istanbul, Turkey. The chapel interior was created by New York designer Charles Lamb. In 1909, Lamb traveled to Rome to enlist the services of six highly accomplished mosaic artists who had just recently completed a project at the Vatican. The artists created more than 10 million mosaic pieces, called tessellae, from marble, colored stone, and glass fused with gold and silver. Lamb's design was inspired by the interior of the San Marco Cathedral in Venice.

The chapel is breathtakingly beautiful with its Byzantine mosaics and religious symbolism. When the sun is just right, it lights up the stained-glass windows, which serve as a sundial telling the time of day and the season, and these words: "Until the day spring breaks and the shadows flee away." The walls are adorned with mosaic figures representing Faith, Hope, Memory, and Love, based on drawings by Ella Condie Lamb, wife of the designer. At the time, the chapel was the only building with an authentic mosaic interior in the United States. It is a wonderful example of Byzantine mosaic art.

The chapel was completed in 1910. The cost of the mosaic work was $150,000, a very large sum at the time. The chapel was dedicated on November 22, 1910, with five of Lakewood's original trustees still on the board. Washburn, its president, addressed the crowd. Through the vision and generosity of the founders, Lakewood continues to exist as a public, non-profit, non-denominational cemetery, considered one of the most beautiful cemeteries in the country.

—*Mary Junge*

MINNESOTA ORCHESTRA ROOTS

Emil Oberhoffer

Among the important area institutions that intersected at its founding with First Universalist was the Minneapolis Symphony Orchestra, renamed the Minnesota Orchestra in 1968. The node connecting the two organizations was the musician Emil Johann Oberhoffer. He assumed the orchestra's podium when it was founded in 1903, at which time he was also the church organist.

Oberhoffer was born into a family of musicians near Munich, Germany, on August 10, 1867. He received extensive musical training in Europe before coming to the United States in the mid-1880s as a young man. According to the story, he and his wife were part of a touring Gilbert and Sullivan troupe that was stranded in St. Paul. He quickly made a mark for himself as a conductor, violinist, composer, pianist and organist. Oberhoffer served as organist and choirmaster of the St. Paul Episcopal Church of St. John the Evangelist in the 1890s, and was a freelance choral conductor.

After leading the Apollo Club and the Schubert Choral Association and Orchestra, he was tapped in 1901 to be the conductor of the Minneapolis Philharmonic Club. Led by Elbert Carpenter, this club gave birth to the Minneapolis Symphony Orchestra. Oberhoffer was on track to become the first conductor of the eighth major orchestra in the United States. Fifty parties signed on as guarantors of the undertaking. Each agreed to contribute up to $200 as needed in case of a deficit against the proposed first year budget of $16,000. The signatories are a Who's Who of the upper crust of Minneapolis in 1903, including First Universalist Society member Thomas Lowry.

Oberhoffer presided over the successful establishment of the orchestra as an artistically respectable and financially viable organization. In 1907, the Orchestral Association of Minnesota was incorporated, taking over from the Philharmonic Club. By 1922, differences with Carpenter reached a breaking point and Oberhoffer stepped down as conductor. After a sold-out last performance, he never conducted the Minneapolis Symphony Orchestra again, though he was in demand as a guest conductor of other major orchestras. First Universalist was fortunate to have had the talents of Oberhoffer as an organist as he also was molding the first edition of what is a world-renowned ensemble.

—*Paul Riedesel*

THE BEGINNINGS: MINISTERS

THE REVEREND JOSEPH WILLARD KEYES, 1864-1866

THE REVEREND JAMES HARVEY TUTTLE, 1866-1891

THE REVEREND MARION DANIEL SHUTTER, 1891-1939

The Beginnings: 1859-1939

Early Ministers

The early members of the church met at several locations after forming in 1859, and heard a series of clergymen. According to a history of the church published by the Reverend James Tuttle in 1891, some of the early traveling ministers who spoke included the Reverends W.W. King, D. M. Reed, and Horace Bushnell.

In the winters of 1863 and 1864, the Reverend Dolphus Skinner of Utica, New York, came to Minneapolis. "His presence in the village was soon known," Tuttle wrote. "He was too earnest and zealous in his profession to remain idle, though he was not physically strong, and the people who were informed of his extraordinary pulpit powers were unwilling to miss the opportunity to hear him."

It was Skinner who would push the young congregation to reorganize and incorporate, which they did in 1864. Shortly thereafter, the Reverend Joseph W. Keyes had his first pastorate here. He was young and fresh from the theological school at Canton, New York. Here he met his future wife, Anna Cooper, a sister of founding member Barclay Cooper. They were married in 1866 by the Reverend Seth Barnes of the First Universalist Society of St. Anthony. Keyes' ministry was only two years, but many new congregants were added during his tenure.

Before he relocated to Rhode Island, Keyes saw the ground-breaking for the First Universalist building on the corner of Fifth Street and Fourth Avenue South. Tuttle described him as "a devoted, excellent preacher" with a "slender constitution" who died soon after leaving Minnesota.

There were "10 cent" evening socials. . . . We always talked about cutting out something else so as not to miss the socials. . . . There was sad news from the [Civil War] front where all had dear ones. The night was bitterly cold, with a raging snowstorm, but we went to Mrs. Birge's for our social. There were 25 present. All said they could not miss it, for where there is great trouble there must be something to relieve it.

— from "Reminiscences" by Mrs. M.S. Staring in *Proceedings of the Celebration of the Fiftieth Anniversary of the Church of the Redeemer*

The Reverend Dolphus Skinner

Though not a settled minister, the Reverend Dolphus Skinner preceded the Reverend Joseph W. Keyes as minister at Woodman Hall, at Washington and Second Avenue South. He performed baptisms and communions, and called together the most interested men and women to incorporate the society in 1864. As described by the Reverend James Tuttle: "He was then a man of perhaps 60, tall, graceful, imposing. . . . He had a rich musical voice. . . . Our pulpit had in that day few finer orators. . . . His tongue dropped manna and thousands fed on it. . . . He could touch the heart as well as convince the intellect."

THE REVEREND JAMES HARVEY TUTTLE

James Harvey Tuttle came to Minneapolis in 1866 in part because of the Great Minnesota Falsehood—the idea, promoted by land speculators, that the Minnesota climate was a cure-all for every kind of ailment.

His wife, Harriet Merriman Tuttle, was in poor health, and both were exhausted after a taxing six-year ministry in Chicago that was strained by the national tumult of the Civil War. When First Universalist's first settled minister, the Reverend Joseph W. Keyes, resigned in poor health, Tuttle accepted an offer to replace him. Thus began a ministry that was to last 25 years. It included the swift growth of the congregation, which outgrew the first building in less than 10 years; the construction of an imposing and ornate stone building dedicated in 1876; its reconstruction after a fire in 1888; and Tuttle's rise to local and national prominence.

Tuttle began life in 1824 as one of 11 children of an upstate New York farmer. The first Tuttles had arrived in Boston in 1635. They were Baptists, but Tuttle became a Universalist in his teens and preached his first sermon at age 18 in a tiny rural church. Despite having had only three years of formal education after elementary school, he was licensed as a Universalist minister at 19. He served a church at Richfield Springs, New York, for three years, and one at Fulton, New York, where he and Harriet Merriman were married in 1848, before moving to Rochester, New York, in 1854 at the age of 30.

Rochester exposed him to a much larger community, a community that included Frederick Douglass, the former slave and abolitionist crusader, and Susan B. Anthony, who fought for women's rights and was a leader in the temperance movement. Both occasionally spoke from his pulpit, and one of those meetings was broken up by a mob of protestors.

It wasn't only the anti-slavery movement that aroused bitter opposition to the church. Universalism itself was condemned by orthodox Christians. The Reverend Marion D. Shutter, Tuttle's assistant and successor at First Universalist, wrote that Universalists "were socially, as well as religiously, ostracized. It was believed that their principles were subversive of common morality, and that, if generally adopted, they would disrupt society." The common idea was that, if there was no hell, there was no incentive to lead a decent life.

Shutter wrote, "It was in Rochester, and under these influences, that Mr. Tuttle reached the conclusion upon which he ever afterwards acted, that Christianity has a social as well as an individual significance, and that its principles are to be applied to the great questions and issues of the day."

Tuttle's arrival at First Universalist in 1866 coincided with the completion of the congregation's first building, at Fifth Street and Fourth Avenue South, where the Government Center parking ramp now stands. It seated 400. The congregation continued to grow so swiftly that the wooden church was supplanted in 1876 by a stone one with pews for 1,000 and a spire whose tip soared more than 200 feet above the sidewalk.

In one of the 12 sermons contained in *The Field and the Fruit,* a memorial volume published when Tuttle retired in 1891, he foreshadowed the aims of First Universalist's social justice efforts a hundred years later: "Christianity is an aggressive religion, an outreaching religion. It is boundlessly comprehensive. Its aims are as wide as the earth. Christianity sends us out of ourselves, out of our homes, out of our churches, out of our [political] parties, out of our nationalities even, on missions of reform; it sends us out of everywhere into everywhere where good is to be done, where the ignorant are to be taught, the hungry fed, the naked clothed, the sorrowful comforted, and transgressors converted."

This philosophy helped to bring rapid growth to the First Universalist Society. Philanthropy also helped. The rich men who dominated

A garden party with the Reverend Tuttle

"Dr. James H. Tuttle was one of the rare men who loved, and was beloved, by all with whom he came in contact. . . . He was a great favorite with the young, especially young lovers. It sometimes seemed to me that they hurried up their matrimonial affairs, that they might have Dr. Tuttle marry them."
—Charles Loring, speaking at the 50th anniversary celebration

"At this period in our Church work a kind Providence sent to us that great and good man, Reverend J.H. Tuttle, a man who in all his useful life did more than any other person I have known to break down the wall of prejudice against the Universalist faith. I believe no man has ever lived who followed more faithfully than Dr. Tuttle the divine injunction, 'Thou shalt love the Lord thy God, with all thy heart and all thy mind and all thy soul and thy neighbor as thyself.' "

—from a letter by Paris Gibson, once First Universalist Sunday School director, later U.S. Senator from Montana, in honor of the 50th anniversary

Minneapolis in the mid-nineteenth century were also the leaders of the church. While they pursued financial success, they also donated generously to First Universalist.

But sorrow also intruded. In 1873 Harriet Merriman Tuttle died in Dresden, Germany, where she had gone with her son in the hope that a sea voyage and another change of climate would restore her health. Tuttle took a year's leave of absence starting in September 1873, to take time to grieve and also "for the purpose of travel in Europe and other Eastern countries." This took him everywhere from Brussels to Rome to Greece, Turkey and Egypt, and places in between. It was the beginning of two decades of travel that informed his sermons and produced travelogues for the *Minneapolis Tribune*.

Tuttle's perceptive eye and natural curiosity were evident no matter where his travels took him. Following a long visit to a logging camp "north of St. Cloud" in 1868, he wrote a comprehensive treatise on the Minnesota logging industry that was published in *Harper*'s magazine. Shutter noted that "it was the first time that the outside world had a glimpse of what was going on in the forests of Minnesota."

Through Tuttle's efforts, a second Universalist church in the community was revitalized in St. Paul. He also spearheaded efforts after retirement to create a third Universalist church, at 27th Street and Blaisdell Avenue South, which eventually became known as the Tuttle Church. It opened in 1894, with a separate congregation and minister, and disbanded in the early 1930s, a victim of the Great Depression. Tuttle's involvement was based on his view that it was important to enlarge the efforts of liberal religion in the new city.

As Shutter wrote about him in 1891: "A minister's work is not to be measured by spasmodic activities, not by phenomenal interest awakened for a few months, not by the applause of the hour, but by permanent results. Time judges all our work, and over that of Dr. Tuttle is written in letters of light, 'Well done!' "

—*John Addington*

THE REVEREND MARION DANIEL SHUTTER

Marion Daniel Shutter served as the pastor of the Church of the Redeemer from 1891 to 1939. Born in New Philadelphia, Ohio, Shutter was the son of a Baptist minister. At age 16, Shutter started college at Denison University in Granville, Ohio, eventually completing his bachelor's and master's degrees at the University of Wooster, Ohio. He began a successful preaching career in Ohio and studied theology at Oberlin and at the Baptist Seminary in Morgan Park, Chicago. After completing his theological studies in 1881, he became the pastor of Olivet Baptist Church in Minneapolis, where he remained for five years, during which time his theology changed. He submitted a letter of resignation, which came to the attention of the Reverend James Tuttle, who suggested he might serve as his assistant at the Church of the Redeemer. Shutter remained in that role for five years and then succeeded Tuttle as pastor in 1891, when Tuttle retired. In the same year, Shutter received his doctor of divinity degree from St. Lawrence University in New York.

One gets the impression that Shutter was larger than life. In his photos, he looks imposing. His sermons show he was a man of strong feelings and opinions. Shutter was an unabashed patriot and deeply suspicious of Socialism. In at least one sermon, he railed against the "Bolsheviki." He represented the Universalist denomination at an international convention of liberals in Paris in 1913 and in Prague in 1927.

Most of his papers reside at Harvard University. He authored six books, including a biography of Tuttle, and collections of essays titled *Justice and Mercy, Wit and Humor in the Bible, A Child of Nature,* and *How the Preachers Pray*. He edited a three-volume history of Minneapolis, and wrote a book titled *Applied Evolution* which sought to integrate the scientific and religious thought of the time. He co-edited *Progressive Men of Minnesota* in 1897, contributing an article titled "Minnesota: Its History and Resources."

Shutter was involved in many aspects of public life in Minneapolis. He was a believer in possibility and was the central figure in founding Unity House in 1897. Along with his wife Mary (Wilkinson), he served on its board until his death in 1939. He was part of a committee to establish public playgrounds. He served as chairman of the Minneapolis Vice

Commission, and later chaired the first Morals Commission. He was honored for his fundraising efforts on behalf of a chapel at Fort Snelling.

In the end, Shutter might have hung on as minister past the time when he should have retired. By the time the Reverend Carl Olson came to replace him, the number of Shutter's congregants was small and dwindling.

As a *Minneapolis Star-Journal* editorial wrote after his death: "Widely informed, gifted with sparkling wit . . . Dr. Shutter might justifiably have claimed the whole city for his parish, and this in a period when the liberalism of his religious credo was deemed by some to be tangential to orthodoxy . . . The last decade had seen him chiefly as a surviving figure of another era. Nonetheless, to a great many families that represent the old-time Minneapolis, he is still institutional to the locale in which he moved for so many active years."

—*Chris Bremer*

Mrs. Mary Shutter (pictured above in 1949) chaired in 1931 the Minnesota chapter of the Women's National Missionary Association effort to raise an endowment for the Clara Barton birthplace in Massachusetts. She played an instrumental role in the Unity House.

Carl Sandburg on Shutter

In his second, unfinished memoir *Ever the Winds of Chance* (1983), poet Carl Sandburg (1878-1967) tells of hearing the Reverend Marion Shutter speak at Lombard College, a Universalist college in Galesburg, Illinois. *He wore a dark gray sack coat, standup collar with corners turned down, and a wide, striped bow tie. His eyes and mouth had subtle and swift changes from utter solemnity to droll and quiet merriment. He hit me deep and was the first preacher to get me saying to myself, "Could it be that my line of work in life ought to be somewhat along his line?"*

Sandburg reports that Shutter came to Lombard in three consecutive years to deliver a series of six lectures. Of his last series, "The Gain to Religious Thought from Scientific Investigation," Sandburg recalled: *Now for the first time in my life I heard the gist and substance of the evidences for evolution, the 'story of the rocks'—those fossil frames of the skeletons of animals, birds, and fishes, having shapes that are vanished from the earth and sea of today—on rock layers even the bones of Early Men and their tools and weapons of stone and later of iron. . . . Over the universe was "a stream of time" where God everlastingly was working changes. This was Dr. Shutter's theme. . . . I was haunted by the thought of how inconceivably old was the earth and all living things on it—and yet at the same moment how fresh and young it all was on that Mayday—and what a long, crooked, wild, and wasteful climb upward it had been from the Early Men to the latest.*

The Beginnings: Members and Leaders

Washburn, Pillsbury, Lowry, Crosby, Loring, King, Morrison.

These are not merely the names of our streets and parks and schools, or the names carved into impressive tombstones at Lakewood Cemetery. They were not only the founders of the Minneapolis flour and lumber industries, of the parks and library system, or supporters of the city's early transportation, the Washburn Orphan Home and the Minneapolis Institute of Arts.

These are the names of the local citizens who long led the First Universalist Society of Minneapolis and Unity House. They found inspiration in the sermons of the Reverends Keyes, Tuttle and Shutter as they fueled the progressive, ground-building programs that put Minneapolis on the map. Following are brief profiles of some of the notable early First Universalists in Minneapolis. All were part of a chain of families that started in Maine, made their fortune and left their legacy in Minneapolis, and are buried in Lakewood Cemetery.

Dorilus (1814-1897) and son Clinton (1842-1913) Morrison
Like their Livermore, Maine, neighbors the Washburns, the Morrison family arrived as lumbering pioneers in 1855. Morrison had a modest beginning, a common school education, starting work with a farmer and tradesman at age 18 for the salary of $7 a month. But it was clear he had a mind for business. He left his employer in his third year when he did not get a raise to $12 a month, but was eventually persuaded to return for $25 a month. He then became a partner in the business, saved $4,000 over five years to launch his own lumbering business, and by 1854 had amassed $20,000, which was what he brought to St. Anthony in 1855.

Morrison, the first mayor of Minneapolis, was a leader who pioneered the development of the dam, canal and water power system of the Mississippi River Falls of St. Anthony. With sons George and Clinton he established the Morrison Brothers saw mills and logging operations, built and sold saw and flour mills along the river, and owned the North Star woolen mill.

Morrison was elected to the Minnesota Senate in 1864, served on the Minneapolis Board of Education for many years, including as its first president, was commissioner of the new park board, and served on the

Thomas Lowry founded the city's earliest transportation system.

Dorilus Morrison was the first editor of the Minneapolis Tribune *and the first mayor of Minneapolis.*

William D. Washburn was involved in a wide variety of civic leadership roles. Washburn helped establish the Northern Pacific Railroad, the Anoka flour mills, and Minneapolis street railway. He was elected to the Minneapolis School Board in 1866, the Minnesota Legislature in 1870, the U.S. House of Representatives in 1878, and the U.S. Senate in 1889.

board of the Athenaeum, precursor to the Minneapolis Public Library. Through it all, the Morrisons, including his son Clinton and his wife, Julie (Washburn), were staunch supporters of First Universalist. Morrison served as president of the Board of Trustees until his death in 1897. He led a committee in 1870 to find property for a new church. Years later, when it was determined that a grander church should be available to people daily, Clinton Morrison and Thomas Lowry led efforts to expand the church in 1903, with donations of $7,000. The younger Morrison, then a church trustee, donated his father's land for the Minneapolis Institute of Arts. In time, Clinton Morrison's daughter Ethel (Van Derlip), also a church member, left a bequest to the Institute's art school.

William D. Washburn (1831 – 1912)

Born to a large Maine family and educated in the East, Washburn was one of four brothers who served in the United States Congress. He came to Minnesota in 1857 to join in his brother Cadwallader's milling operation—the eventual General Mills company—and invested his entrepreneurial spirit and growing financial assets into civic service. He presided over the founding meeting of the First Universalist Society of Minneapolis in 1859, served on the church's Board of Trustees for its first 50 years, even after he was elected Senator, and had the financial resources to give an expensive organ to the first church building in 1866, and a bell tower for the second building in 1876.

Excerpted from *History of the City of Minneapolis, Minnesota* (1898)

The Soo, as the Minneapolis, Sault Ste. Marie and Atlantic railway line is popularly denominated, is in conception and realization of the Washburn family. Gov. Israel Washburn addressed the citizens of Minneapolis, advocating for the facilitating of their trade, the construction of a railway line. …The conception remained to fructify and take bodily shape when his brother, W. D. Washburn … pushed it to completion in an incredibly short time … to serve the large milling interests of Minneapolis, and the producers of the Northwest, by opening up a new and competing line to the East. …Like all his distinguished brothers, he had a taste for politics, and like them belonged to the radical wing of the Republican party. Strongly anti-slavery in the ante-bellum days, when that was an engrossing political question… he took ground against the importation of Chinese laborers…He was a protectionist in theory…Through his influence, the national government erected a fine building for the Federal courts and post office in Minneapolis, and undertook the system of reservoirs at the sources of the Mississippi.

Caroline Macomber Crosby (1871–1960)

The Reverend Marion Shutter and the trustees of the Church of the Redeemer recruited Caroline Crosby to be head resident of Unity House in 1904. They knew what they were doing. For 13 years, she brought her considerable volunteer energies to helping develop free kindergarten, a Mothers' Club, a day nursery, a sewing school, library, gymnasium, and a probation office connected with the juvenile court to oversee 81 boys and 7 girls.

After taking on her role at Unity House, Crosby became a central figure in the philanthropy of the Crosby family. Many of the people served by Unity House were members of families that worked in the Washburn-Crosby Mills, later known as General Mills, founded by her father, John Crosby. Many of those who helped to create Unity House were from the privileged mining families. In addition to serving as head resident, Crosby was a major contributor to the annual budget.

Caroline Crosby

Crosby left Unity House to serve in the Red Cross during World War I, then went on to positions with the Children's Protective Society, the Infant Welfare Society, and the Children's Home Society. In 1934 she followed a life-long interest and traveled to New Zealand and Australia to collect algae.

Alfred Fiske Pillsbury (1869-1950) and Eleanor (Field) Pillsbury (died 1946)

Longtime Unity House board member, Eleanor Field Pillsbury was active in the church by 1906, when she co-chaired the Women's Association Publishing Fund committee. By 1913 her husband Alfred Fiske Pillsbury, son of Governor John Pillsbury and co-founder of Pillsbury Mills, served as vice president of the church board. He was named president emeritus after more than 15 years of presidential service. Pillsbury was deeply involved in Minneapolis activities: the parks, fine arts, symphony, transportation, and banks. Described as one of the first great football players at the University of Minnesota, Pillsbury also owned the city's first high-wheeled bicycles, one of its first three automobiles, and had one of the western world's best Chinese bronze and jade collections, donated to the Minneapolis Institute of Arts. In 1887, other Pillsbury members included Miss Minnie Pillsbury and Mrs. Francis B. Pillsbury.

Alfred Pillsbury

—*Mikki Morrissette with contributions by the Reverend Sarah Barber-Braun*

The funeral of the last surviving founding member, Barclay Cooper, held in 1938 at Church of the Redeemer

Memorial to Founding Member Barclay Cooper (1842-1938)

Most members of the church were not the notable movers and shakers of the city, but simple men, women and children who raised families, held jobs, and found spiritual community in the Universalist faith. The last surviving founding member was laid to rest with the words of the Reverend Marion Shutter on April 7, 1938, from whose tribute this information comes.

Barclay Cooper was born October 23, 1842, to Milton and Zillah (Preston) Cooper, Quakers in Lancaster County, Pennsylvania. He was the fourth of seven children. They migrated by train to Chicago (that leg took eight days), by steamer to St. Paul, and by stagecoach to Minneapolis, arriving in 1857. He often said that the depression of 1857 was much worse than the depression of 1930 and 1936.

As a young man, Cooper cut cordwood in Kenwood, built sailboats on Lake Calhoun, studied the Indians, and eventually joined—and then ran —his father's construction firm to help build Nicollet Hotel, the first apartment buildings in Minneapolis, and the Metropolitan Opera House. He married Miss Adelaide Bassett on September 14, 1869, in Ohio.

At the first meeting of the church in 1859, Cooper attended with his sisters Amy, Elvira and Anna, who signed the book as charter members. After the first church building was erected, Cooper served as Sunday School librarian and sang with his sisters in the choir. Although he opposed war, having been raised a Quaker, Cooper enlisted in 1864 and engaged in battles in Tennessee.

"Serene in spirit, he was not disturbed by the tumults of the world, for he knew that God reigned and that the storms would cease. This picture of him remains with me. I shall never forget how, at a beautiful baptismal service at the Lake last summer, he lovingly held his great-grandchild on his knee—a tiny bud of springtime gathered to the warmth of his autumnal heart."

Women's Organizations

Nineteenth-century women were identified by their husband's names—Mrs. Tuttle, Mrs. Shutter, Mrs. Andrews—or their father's—and their work was more behind the scenes than from the pulpit or podium. However, First Universalist women knew how to get things done, and within 10 years of the founding of the church, they had organized the Ladies Social Circle. This group raised $8,000 to help build and furnish the new church building of 1876, and was central to the success of Unity House.

Branching off from the social circle in 1904, the Women's Association was later incorporated in 1907. It was created to connect with the Women's National Missionary Association. They conducted the sewing school at Unity House, helped pay for Unity's probation officer, published and distributed monthly pastoral sermons, and formed the Pastor's Aid and Sunday School committees. The women tended to meet around serious topics, chosen to "broaden our view of humanity and its needs," such as child labor (according to the 1910 yearbook). In 1920, the year women got the right to vote, three speakers talked to the group about suffrage.

The women's work was rooted in social reform and charity. In the early 1900s they made a habit of donating pennies equal to their age once a year for a single good cause.

After Mildred Olson came to Minneapolis in 1939 with her husband, the Reverend Carl Olson, she merged the two groups into the Association of Universalist Women (AUW).

William Eastman, who died in 1908, left one-fourth of his estate to carry on the charitable works of the Church of the Redeemer. His wife was described by Mrs. M.S. Staring, in the book commemorating the first 50 years, as a woman whose "heart and hand and purse were always open."

As of 1905, the Ladies Social Circle had raised $32,000, which was used for church repairs and furnishings ($17,217); aid work ($3,035); missionary contributions to divinity students and conventions ($2,761); Unity House ($2,784).

By the end of 1912, 56,000 copies of Shutter sermons had been distributed with the help of the Women's Association.

Gambling for the Church

To raise money to furnish the new church, the Ladies Social Circle held a week-long New England Dinner and Fair at Brackett's Hall. As the Hon. William P. Roberts reported at the 50th anniversary celebration in 1909, "All sorts of schemes, booths, etc., were run to turn an honest penny for the church—even to grab-bags, lotteries, chances and other gambling devices. I am glad to say, however, that that was the very last time such practices were ever countenanced. Dr. Tuttle disapproved and his wishes were observed."

MARY GARARD ANDREWS (1853-1936)

AUW activist Mary Garard Andrews was an important local and national figure in the woman suffrage movement, the temperance movement and the Universalist denomination and was one of the first women ministers in the United States.

Andrews was highly independent and mobile for a woman of her time. She was born in West Virginia in 1853, supported herself after being orphaned at the age of 12 and attended two of the first colleges to admit women in Michigan and Illinois—one while she held her first ministerial job at the Free Will Baptist Church in Hillsdale, Michigan.

She soon converted to Universalism and was ordained as a Universalist minister in 1881. She served Universalist churches in Nebraska, Iowa and Illinois and continued working part-time after marrying Isaac R. Andrews. She graduated from Lombard in 1887 with a bachelor of divinity degree. Her thesis was "The Influence of [Unitarian William Ellery] Channing Upon American Theology."

By 1910, six years after her husband's death, Andrews and her son, Rollin, settled in Minneapolis, where she joined Church of the Redeemer and became active in the Women's Association and the statewide Women's Missionary Association. She also joined the Equal Suffrage Association, the Political Equality Club, the Lewis Parliamentary Law Association, the Columbian Club, the Minneapolis Society of Fine Arts, the Women's Co-operative Alliance, and the Business and Professional Women's Club.

Andrews helped direct the Caroline Crosby Club at Unity House, a weekly literary meeting, which in 1910 discussed "The Conflict of Color: the White, the Black, the Yellow," "Conservation of Health," "China's Awakening" and "The Immigration Problem."

After her death in 1936 her son remained a member of First Universalist Church and served on the Board of Trustees, including as president.

I never spent much time with the oft controversial question, 'Shall women preach?' I thought the most satisfactory solution of the problem would be for each woman quietly, without ostentation or controversy, to assume her place and let her work speak for itself.

—Mary Garard Andrews

—information from *100 Years of Liberation: Association of Universalist Women, Minneapolis,* 1905-2005, and Yearbook, Church of the Redeemer, Minneapolis, 1910

The Beginnings: 1859-1939

UNITY HOUSE

The settlement work in north Minneapolis has done more than anything in our history to stimulate our interest in something outside of ourselves and give an outlet to our energies.

—the Reverend Marion Shutter, 1899 annual report

Unity House was established in Minneapolis on September 21, 1897, by a group of religiously liberal ministers led by the Reverend Marion Shutter of the Church of the Redeemer. In the 75th anniversary booklet of the church, published in 1934, Unity House was said to have stemmed from initial support to establish a kindergarten on the north side that Shutter and the church had pledged to support. But the inspiration likely came from Shutter's visit to the original model for settlement houses, Toynbee Hall in London, England.

Unity House provided kindergarten for 100 children by 1907.

The settlement house movement has been called "the first war on poverty." Unity House in Minneapolis was set up as a secular settlement house with a secular mission from the start, but it soon became identified as a project of the Universalist congregation with significant volunteer involvement from the church. One feature after another developed.

In 1898, just six and a half months after the founding of Unity House, the following accomplishments were reported:
- A kindergarten with full enrollment of 56 children
- A Mothers' Club (32 attendees)
- A day nursery
- A penny savings program (65 children)
- A program affiliated with the public library (100 children)
- Evening classes (70 students)
- Lectures by University of Minnesota professors
- A boys' club (115 members)
- Plans for a girls' club

By 1911, Unity House served 543 young women in 12 clubs ranging from sewing classes to literary clubs.

Twenty of the one-time 140 members of the Unity House Mothers' Club gathered in 1958 to celebrate its 60-year anniversary. One of those women was Mrs. Gertrude Bretz, 76, who had been a member for 57 years. Her mother was a charter member of the club. Bretz recalled that in the earliest days members brought their own cup and spoon for refreshments. In 1916 the group successfully protested the development of a garbage station in the neighborhood. They promoted a dental clinic at Unity House, and were regular contributors to the Red Cross.

Although it was eventually embroiled in an IRS tax issue, the boys' club pool hall was a benefit for city youth.

Evening programs included academic classes and vocational training opportunities. Professors from the university taught classes in U.S. history, mechanical drawing, bookkeeping and free-hand drawing. These classes were available to people who worked during the day and to those who were too old to attend the public schools. Elementary-age students could get help with reading, spelling, and arithmetic. By the end of 1898, the girls' club had been established, as well as a girls' sewing class and a men's debating club.

Initially, Unity House was at 1616 Washington Avenue North. Over the next 14 years it expanded, and by 1911 the original building became the Headquarters and Girls' Building, with a playground across the street, a

library and gymnasium at the corner of 17th Avenue North and Third Street, a boys' club at 1714 North Third Street, and a boys' boarding club at 1705 North Fifth Street.

From 1904 to 1915, the head resident at Unity was Church of the Redeemer member Caroline Crosby, of the Crosby milling family. Under her unpaid leadership, the staff at Unity grew from 3 to 13, with several changes in facilities.

Most of the other staff members at Unity House were university students, many of whom were studying for careers in social work or recreation. A few went on to prominence: Koyama Matsu San later operated a similar program in Japan; George White and Elsie Hossly helped develop the American College in Greece; and Milo Christianson became supervisor of recreation for Washington, D.C. Locally, Edward Currie went on to work at Pillsbury House, and his sister Constance Currie became director of Neighborhood House in St. Paul.

The Shutters were deeply involved in the operation of Unity House for decades and helped maintain its practical focus.

After the 1930s, Unity and the other settlement houses in Minneapolis evolved into community centers for neighborhood-based social and recreational services. As time went on, there was less focus on helping recent immigrants and more attention given to the needs of low-income families in general.

Throughout its existence, Unity House programs continued to include the sewing and woodworking classes that it started during its first year. Among Unity's other programs was an employment bureau for women, which continued for several decades to help neighborhood women find household work. When church members needed help with house-cleaning, they would go to Unity to hire someone. In a time before publicly funded financial assistance existed for those in poverty, this provision of temporary work opportunities was seen as a way to help struggling families.

In 1923 and 1924, the not-yet-famous actor Henry Fonda lived and worked at Unity House while a student at the University of Minnesota. As his biography reported: "I'd coach softball or touch football .. basketball or track or swimming. . . . After dinner there'd be three games of basketball. By 11:30, I'd get to my room and homework for the next day. Every night, I'd fall asleep over my books, dead tired . . . At the end of my sophomore year I was so exhausted that when they passed out the blue books for the final exams, I just sat in class and drew pictures instead of answering the questions. I flunked out of Minnesota."

In 1910, as probation officer at Unity House, Caroline M. Macomber reported:

- 81 boys on probation during year;
- 21 girls on probation during year;
- 8 boys sent to juvenile detention home;
- 23 dependent children;
- 972 calls made;
- 135 letters written;
- 19 for whom employment found.

She wrote: "It is worthy of record that the Church of the Redeemer is the only church in the city that has supplied a probation officer . . . The playgrounds, the clubs, the classes and the gymnasium give a wholesome outlet for activities that would otherwise be misdirected. Much of my work is preventive. . . . Of 669 different children on probation in the city during the year, only 101 were from our district."

Eventually, Unity House even offered a farming project that, in its seventh year, served more than 200 children over the age of 12. The program was lauded by the Minnesota Department of Labor and Industry in a 1949 letter, which indicated that the counseling given by Unity to the young workers about wage and hour standards had contributed to "significant gains in the raising of child labor standards."

In 1968, Unity House was sold and torn down to make way for freeway development. Part of the proceeds from the sale were used to fund programs located in north Minneapolis at the time of the sale. The remainder was used to create the First Universalist Foundation in 1984.

The most innovative and well-thought-of programs that Unity started were quickly subsumed by publicly funded institutions. The kindergarten and evening classes were taken over by the public schools. Similarly, the health care, social work, and juvenile probation services started at Unity were also brought into the public sector. Gymnasiums, pools, playgrounds, and childcare became much more available within the larger fabric of the community. Unity House helped to show the value of these programs to the entire community and demonstrated that people of faith could make a lasting difference in their community.

—*Chris Bremer*

The Beginnings: 1859-1939   27

Camp Unity

Each summer starting in 1906, children at Unity House were invited to spend time at camp at Lake Independence near Loretto, Minnesota. Starting in 1910 the destination became Lake Wapogasset near Amory, Wisconsin. Activities included: toothbrush drill, campfires, vaudeville night, clean tent competition, swimming, fishing and boating.

Church Homes

The 1876 dedication of Church of the Redeemer (right) at Eighth Street and Second Avenue, as reported in local newspapers:

"A fairer day than last Sunday never smiled on God's green earth. A trifle warm, perhaps, but the sky was cloudless, and the blazing orb of day rode through the heavens in majestic splendor, while all Nature beamed with joy and gratitude."

Reportedly hundreds were turned away because of overcapacity. "It was such an outpouring of the religious community, as we do not remember to have heretofore witnessed in this city."

Commenting on the sermon of one of the three speakers, Dr. A.A. Miner of Boston, one reporter wrote, "In common with that vast audience, he was lost to everything save the eloquent speaker and his theme, and his pencil forgot its duty until the last word was spoken."

After the first organizational meeting at the Cataract House, the new congregation met at Harrison Hall at Nicollet and Washington and Woodman Hall at Washington and Second Avenue. It took seven years for the congregation to build its first church, in 1866, at Fifth Street and Fourth Avenue South. Built in a Gothic style, it included the first complete church organ in the city, made of black walnut.

As the Reverend James Tuttle would later describe it, "This new temple would seem humble enough now, doubtless, but it was worth the much enthusiastic pride we took in it then. It was centrally located, convenient, large enough for the time, and not without architectural attractions. It seated about 400, and was generally well filled, often crowded."

Eight years later this church was sold to the German Methodists. Plans were made to erect a new church of native blue limestone, after raising $40,000. The new structure was built at a somewhat far-flung location—Eighth Street and Second Avenue South—and was dedicated July 10, 1876, as the Church of the Redeemer, reportedly named after a Chicago church that Tuttle admired. It cost more than $70,000, had damask pew

The Beginnings: 1859-1939

cushions, and richly carved wood paneling. Another gift from trustee William D. Washburn was a bell tower in 1882.

On January 15, 1888, the church was swept by fire. As the Reverend Marion Shutter wrote in his *History of Minneapolis,* "Great volumes of smoke issued from all parts of the great temple for hours. . . . The roof fell in late in the afternoon. The thick, heavy walls, covered with hanging masses of ice remained. . . . The Congregational, Methodist, Unitarian and Jewish people at once offered the use of their places of worship, but . . . the bereaved members . . . decided to announce that they would hold services for awhile in the Grand Opera House."

Member Mrs. Louise Morgan Lovejoy reported: "It was one of the coldest of Minnesota's cold days. . . . The tower clock moved its faithful hands around as usual and struck every hour, sounding out solemnly through the dark tempest raving about it until 4 p.m., when, clothed with frost, it stopped. . . . A considerable part of the Sunday School library was tossed through the windows on to the snow."

The Reverend Carl Olson would report later, "Strangely enough, the Communion service, locked in an oak cabinet in the pastor's study, was rescued days later and showed no touch of fire or taint of smoke. They are still in possession of the church."

The church's 212-foot bell tower survived the fire, as did some of the wall that formed the framework for the rebuilt larger building, which was dedicated on November 24, 1889.

Large memorial windows, created by Tiffany and Herter Brothers, commemorated members of the early families of Morrison, Rand, Coykendall, Tuttle, Gilson, Herrick and Washburn. As long-time member Major William D. Hale said at the church's 50th anniversary celebration: "It would be a dull soul indeed who could sit through a service in the light streaming through their richly blended colors and not be uplifted to nobler resolve and purer life. I have sometimes

January 15, 1888, the Church of the Redeemer went up in flames (above) and was shrouded in frost (below) a day later.

thought that Dr. Shutter might have reason to be jealous of the distracting influence of those voiceless 'sermons in stones.' But what cares he through what channel the waiting soul is reached?"

In 1903, the windows were destroyed in a tornado. They were later restored.

With the intent of developing a centrally located modern church that was open every day of the week, the Church of the Redeemer was expanded in 1903 to provide three additional rooms, including a church office. Much of the $7,000 in funds were provided by long-time members and business associates Thomas Lowry and Clinton Morrison. Mrs. Shutter raised more than $2,000 for furnishings.

In a report to trustees in 1915, Shutter wrote: "While it may not be immediate, the question of another location for our Church building is again brought to the front by the purchase of the entire block diagonally across from us by the Street Railway Company, for terminals. It may be that, in spite of the

Tuttle presented the church with a replica of an angel christening font designed in marble by Thorwaldsen of Copenhagen, which he had seen during a vacation to Europe. The font was given to Our Lady of Lourdes Catholic Church in 1970.

The restored Church of the Redeemer featured an $11,000 organ, with hand-carved vines, flowers and choir boys, designed by Pelzer, sculptor for the first Kaiser Wilhelm. It was a gift from William D. Washburn.

desirability of maintaining a central position, business may at last force us out. ... I have a chart in my office which indicates the distribution of our constituents. A fair proportion is scattered over the outlying districts, on the East Side, far to the north, and around the Lakes. The present location is on the very edge of our territory. Fully one-fourth of our people live upon the Lowry Hill side of Hennepin Avenue, and the larger part of the remaining three-fourths, in a district bounded by Eighth Street, Chicago Avenue, 34th Street, and Hennepin Avenue."

Eventually, as the growing population of Minneapolis' moved continually southward, and the automobile made transportation into newer neighborhoods and suburbs easier, church members found new places of worship. Descendants of church pioneers "married into the orthodox churches," according to long-time church staff person Marion Griffith.

By the time of Shutter's death in 1939, Sunday services attracted perhaps 30 remaining elderly congregants, a tiny fraction of the 900-person capacity of the sanctuary. The trustees had been looking for a buyer for the building as early as 1926, and found its chance to sell the Church of the Redeemer in 1941 to the Catholic Archdiocese, for $112,500. Eventually the original building burned on Ash Wednesday 1953, although the bells from the tower were saved.

—*Mikki Morrissette with contributions by John Addington*

Misunderstanding

First Universalist did not have its beginnings in the church building now known as Our Lady of Lourdes Catholic Church on the east bank of the Mississippi River, although the plaque in front of the building says it was built by the First Universalist Church. It was the First Universalist Society of St. Anthony, not of Minneapolis. St. Anthony was annexed to Minneapolis in 1872. In that same year, the building was sold to the Catholics after the Universalist congregation disintegrated following the heresy trial of its minister, the Reverend Herman Bisbee, also in 1872. Bisbee had clashed with the Reverend James Tuttle over Bisbee's support for Charles Darwin and was removed from fellowship by the Universalist organization because he invaded Tuttle's territory by crossing the river to deliver a series of lectures attacking Tuttle's anti-evolutionary views. Bisbee was the only Universalist minister removed from fellowship for heresy.

The Tuttle Church

The downtown Church of the Redeemer included some of the city's wealthiest families. The Reverend James Tuttle also wanted to minister to the less prosperous. After his retirement in 1891, he focused energy on a satellite church at 27th Street and Blaisdell, which officially was the Third Universalist Society of Minneapolis but became known as Tuttle Memorial Universalist Church after his death.

Marion Griffith, long-time church secretary who started out at Tuttle Church, remembered it as "kind of a little mission church. The one downtown was where the rich people went. The Tuttle Church was ordinary people."

The Tuttle building was so named because of the tireless efforts of Tuttle to help it succeed. Before his death, he asked his successor, the Reverend Marion Shutter, to help raise funds if an expansion should be needed someday. This happened in 1914, with $5,000 raised from Church of the Redeemer congregants in order to help the growth of liberal religion in the city.

Following economic difficulties, the Tuttle Church began to decline in 1921. By August 1931, regular services were discontinued. Eventually many members of Tuttle Church—which included the families of E.H. Scofield, George D. Crocker, George L. Cornell, and Griffith—joined the Church of the Redeemer.

MOVING FORWARD: 1939-2009

This picture of the congregation was taken at Church House at 4600 Dupont Avenue on July 5, 1942. The Reverend Carl Olson is bottom right with son Robert and daughter Margaret.

As a house where many shall find that truth which makes us free;
as a place of light, we set apart this house . . .
As a house where many shall dedicate themselves to the cause of perpetual good;
as a place of goodwill, we set apart this house . . .
As a house where many shall find that divine presence which is our solemn joy and hope according as
it is our continual devotion; as a place of joy we set apart this house . . .
To that life, that it may carry blessing to many people, even unto generations yet unborn, we offer this
building; to the service of mankind we dedicate this church.

—Words spoken at the dedication service on October 23, 1949, for the new church building
at 5000 Girard Avenue South, in honor of First Universalist's 90th anniversary

MOVING FORWARD

GROWTH AND ACTIVISM

The cornerstone-laying ceremony for the church at 5000 Girard Avenue South, on May 23, 1948, included the placement of a time capsule of the church history in a corner of the building.

The Reverend Marion Shutter's pastorate spanned 48 years, from the church's young adulthood to what seemed like its old age. By 1939, when he died, the rich and powerful founders were long gone, and most of their descendants had found other church attachments. Improved transportation had changed living patterns in Minneapolis, and people tended to worship where they lived, increasingly far from downtown. As few as 30 people might be found in the 1,000-seat Church of the Redeemer sanctuary on Eighth Street on a Sunday.

After the Reverend Carl Olson came in 1939, the diminished congregation sold the downtown building to the Catholic Archdiocese in 1941 and made plans for a new building in south Minneapolis—just before the bombing of Pearl Harbor. The congregation banked the sale money and waited out the war in a large house at 4600 Dupont Avenue South, which became known as Church House.

The tiny church could have faded away, but First Universalists are a resilient, determined people. As the hymn says, "we are a gentle, angry people . . . a justice seeking people . . . a gentle, loving people," and we were singing for our lives. In 1949 the growing congregation moved into its new building at 5000 Girard Avenue South and began a vibrant era of the church's history.

This section, *Moving Forward,* is a look at the second half of the 150 years of First Universalist Church, a time of growth and activism that saw Universalists merge with Unitarians and a renewed commitment to being a creative presence in the city, the state, the denomination and the world.

Moving Forward: 1939-2009

THE TIMES

Minneapolis was no longer an isolated frontier town in 1939, and First Universalists along with the rest of the world were just emerging from the trauma of the Great Depression. They had seen the war to end all wars, or so they thought. On December 7, 1941, the plan to construct a new church would be thwarted by the bombing of Pearl Harbor and the entry of the United States into World War II. There were no building materials for churches in wartime.

The Reverend Carl Olson, with trustees Rollin Andrews and Robert Pugh, preside over the burning of the mortgage after the church was able to get out of debt in 1952.

Events half a world away were beginning to affect the daily lives of Minneapolitans, a situation that increased exponentially each decade of the twentieth century. The Reverend Carl Olson began each worship hour with thoughts and prayers for First Universalists in the armed services, and also decried the spread of communism from the pulpit. Two decades later, the Reverend John Cummins marched in Selma, Alabama, with Dr. Martin Luther King, Jr., and counseled conscientious objectors during the Vietnam War.

Universalist women had always been active, but the feminist movement that gained momentum after the publication of Betty Friedan's *The Feminine Mystique* perhaps eased Myrna Hansen's election as president of the Board of Trustees in 1965, the first woman in 106 years of church history to hold that position.

The congregation's world view was altered in ways unimaginable in 1859, forever changed by the horror of two world wars and the holocaust; by the dropping of the atomic bomb; by the scourge of AIDS; by the naming of ancient injustices in terms of race and gender and sexual orientation and the imperative to right those wrongs; by a string of assassinations; and by the terrorist attacks on September 11, 2001.

The way we lived was also affected by scientific and technological advances that improved health, created a host of labor-saving machines, made transportation quick, communication instantaneous, and food from all over the world available at our

Finding a sense of connectedness by joining hands at the conclusion of worship service.

First Universalist members continued to be active in civic as well as church life. Nancy Atchison was elected to the Edina School Board; Tom Berg to the state legislature; Joan Niemic and Carol Johnson to the Minneapolis City Council; Helen Meyer was appointed to the Minnesota Supreme Court; Mark Ritchie was elected Minnesota Secretary of State.

local grocery store. *Local* took on new meaning; the interdependent web of life was made obvious.

Embracing the new technological world wasn't easy. In 1985 the board boldly decided that the church should invest in a computer, and trustee Karin Wille hosted a fundraiser to raise the $6,000 needed —a huge sum. It was a momentous and somewhat controversial decision, and not entirely welcomed by church staff who would have to learn to use the thing. But, by 2009 First Universalist Church had a website with numerous links; a chat group called Cyber Coffeehour and a weekly CyberNews; an electronic edition of *The Liberal* newsletter; a computer on every desk in the church; a sesquicentennial website; and a new minister, the Reverend Justin Schroeder who included a "Technology and Ministry" page in his ministerial packet.

By the end of the twentieth century the reality of world citizenship was evident on many levels of church life. First Universalist youth traveled to Poland and Nicaragua in the Youth Cultural Exchange, and Polish and Nicaraguan young people came to First Universalist. New waves of immigrants, particularly Somali and Hmong, were served by the First Universalist Foundation and participated in the Unity Leadership Institute. The church protested the war in Iraq and celebrated the family of Lewis Bishop when he was sent to Iraq in 2009.

As the congregation was increasingly affected by and involved in global issues, there was a need for connection on a micro level: people were hungry for community. Ministers and congregants introduced new elements to services and to communal and individual rituals. But the congregation also needed a sense of community, of connectedness, of knowing who it is together.

Perhaps that is why this story of the 150-year history was so important and so compelling in 2009. Knowing stories in context enables a community to know who it is as a people, how it got to this bend in the road, and to have a sense of where the road might go. First Universalists join hands at the end of worship service, and sing "Go Now in Peace," to stay connected and strong and to be filled with the joy and possibility of the spirit of life.

— *Kathy Coskran*

The Reverend Carl Olson (1939-1963)

The Reverend Carl Harold Olson was what business observers today call a turn-around artist. He became minister of a greatly diminished Church of the Redeemer in 1939 and, in the course of 24 years, presided over what a more conservative denomination might describe as a resurrection.

On a Sunday morning that first year a visitor would find maybe 30 people, most of them middle-aged and older, in a sanctuary that seated 1,000. It was a sad comedown for a once-thriving church. Its pioneers were gone. The Reverend Marion Shutter, the minister who had served the congregation since becoming assistant minister in 1886 and senior minister in 1891, had just died in office at the age of 86. The Great Depression and changing demographics had reduced church membership to fewer than a hundred.

Olson's decision to move from ministry in a small Ohio church to the once and future big one in Minneapolis was a daunting step, but he was used to being undaunted. He was born in Quincy, Massachusetts, the son of a policeman who died at an early age. Olson worked his way through Tufts University, earning a Phi Beta Kappa key in his junior year, and prepared for the Universalist ministry at Crane Theological School in Boston. He was encouraged to come west by the Reverend Robert Cummins, general superintendent of the Universalist Church of America. It may have figured into the thinking of both men that a minister with a Swedish name would have a head start in the Swedish capital of the nation.

Carl and Mildred Olson with their daughter Margaret at their 25th wedding anniversary.

When Olson arrived, it was obvious that Church of the Redeemer could no longer afford the big, ornate stone building at Eighth Street and Second Avenue South in downtown Minneapolis. The solution came in 1941 when the Catholic Archdiocese wanted to establish a downtown parish and bought the building. The proceeds were to be used to build a new church in south

Minneapolis, nearer the geographical center of its membership, but Pearl Harbor intervened. Building materials went mostly to the war effort. The congregation took up temporary, cramped residence at a house at 4600 Dupont Avenue, which became known as Church House.

On April 3, 1949, First Universalist was finally able to dedicate its new church building at 5000 Girard Avenue South. The Reverend Robert Cummins preached the dedicatory sermon.

The Reverend Carl Olson, at his installation service at Church of the Redeemer, December 1, 1939.

Under Olson's leadership the membership steadily increased. By the time of his retirement in 1963, because of ill health, it totaled 450 adults and 600 children.

In addition to leading the church's revival, Olson served as a national trustee of the Universalist Church of America. Among his many civic duties, he was a director of Family and Children's Service, chairman of Minneapolis' first urban redevelopment commission and a member of the state labor arbitration panel. He also lectured at the University of Minnesota Law School and served on the Minnesota Governor's Human Rights Commission and its predecessor, the Interracial Commission.

A few weeks prior to his arrival in Minneapolis, Olson wrote to church secretary Marion Griffith: "I have never been installed! It has been one of those things which I have wanted to reserve for the place in which it would appear my best work would be done. And now I am quite happy to have this initial experience in Minneapolis. December first will be the tenth anniversary of my ordination. Would this not be an appropriate date?"

—*John Addington*

Olson on God

"There are some who so emphatically reject the commonly accepted connotations of the word that they . . . reject the word itself. . . . Almost all Universalists . . . admitting their own limitations of knowledge, accept the physicists' statement that the universe is composed of units of energy. This energy does eventuate in objects that are separate and unique. And the principle of power or spirit by which this energy is grouped into patterns or configurations that give us this world in a form apprehensible by humans may properly be called God."

Letter-writing to Our Soldiers

The Reverend Carl Olson was a loyal letter-writer to World War II troops—a practice his predecessor, the Reverend Marion Shutter, had engaged in as well. As one soldier, Leslie Snyder, wrote in a letter to Shutter in 1918, after receiving a letter and "one of those inspiring sermons which I have many times longed to hear once more," he "forgot for the moment the cold rain outside, the puddles of water, the mud, ankle deep, and the monotonous rows of barracks, and pictured myself seated in the rear of the church with the organ playing and the choir singing their Christmas carols."

This image of George Betzler is in our church archives.

In a letter dated June 27, 1942, Olson said he'd like to write more often, and would "if there were not sermons to prepare, a new baby to see." He said they were checking addresses of returned letters. "Some of you move around more than a Methodist parson." On June 9, 1943, he reported that the newly merged AUW would add a brief greeting to each letter going out, since he hadn't been able to keep up. "People here are working at victory gardens. . . . Margaret (4-1/2) has just come into the study and says, 'I would like to ask the soldiers 'How are you today?' She'll have a lot more in a minute or two, so we'll sign off right away! Otherwise she will be asking for military secrets."

On May 1, 1946, after four years of monthly letters, Olson wrote: "This is to be my last mimeographed letter to men in service from our Church. Because of this, it is being sent to everyone —including those already discharged—so that all may be 'in' on the conclusion of what appears to have been a unique contact between a church and its people in service. It was long ago—and even in another 'age'—that these monthly letters were begun. At first, as some of you can recall, I wrote individual letters. It was quite a job and soon it became clear that I'd have to change this or give up preparing Sunday sermons . . . It was a puzzle—and then there came the bright idea of writing a master-letter to everyone and of having it duplicated, fifty copies at a whack! Miss Griffith gladly agreed to handle the mimeographing as her part in a war-time project.

"Since this is something of a review, I'll add mention of the 'Quiz Sheet' which was sent with each letter beginning a few months later. This sheet of tricks and questions, it seemed to me, might interest you and furnish you with recreational material at times and in places where there might be nothing of the sort available. So it proved, for your letters told me of quiz sheets—and the letters themselves—being shared with others in all theatres of war and in all stages of the conflict. (Incidentally, a magazine for servicemen, *Link*, requested permission to reprint our quiz sheet.)"

Although Olson was discontinuing the practice of mimeographed letters, since so many men were being discharged, "It really means that we go back to the old system of individual letters, for I've answered your personal letters all along." He then went on to list information about all who had been or were still in service from the church, including two who lost their lives—Curtiss Record Hayes and John King—and 50 other men (such as Lynn Elling, transporting discharges across the country) and one woman, Verna Harris, living in Texas with "THE man" she met at an Indiana hospital.

The Reverend John Cummins (1963-1986)

When the Reverend John Cummins, minister of First Universalist Church from 1963 to 1986, arrived in Minneapolis, the *Minneapolis Tribune* described him as a "tweedy New Englander" because he often wore a tweed jacket with felt patches on the elbows. But that was wrong, says Cummins, who was born in Ohio in 1926, three weeks after his father, the Reverend Robert Cummins, was ordained as a Universalist minister. Being a preacher's kid greatly influenced his adult life. "A whole string of interesting guests came through our home, so I was always aware of what was going on in the world," he says. "I was never a normal American kid. While other kids were playing baseball in a corner sandlot, I was listening to Gandhi's speeches on the radio about liberating India."

Cummins received his bachelor of arts degree in 1947 from Bowdoin College. At that time the Universalist Church of America had two major sources of ministers: St. Lawrence University in New York state and Tufts University in Boston. Because his father was head of the Universalist Church of America, Cummins felt pressure from both institutions to attend their divinity school. "So I went to Harvard," he said. Cummins graduated in 1950 and was ordained by his father on June 4 of that year.

Cummins' first congregation was a struggling little church in Brunswick, Maine, which had no minister's study and no running water. "I fired the furnace on Saturday night, ran out in the country and collected farm kids on Sunday morning, played the piano for Sunday school, then rang the bell for church and went down and preached the sermon," he said. The best thing that came out of that experience was meeting his wife, Drusilla, whom he married in August 1951. In 1954, Cummins moved to a church in Waltham, Massachusetts. He also served as chaplain at Brandeis University for a time and in 1963, moved to Minneapolis to become the fifth settled minister for the 104-year-old First Universalist Church.

From the beginning it was clear that Cummins was not afraid of controversy. Within 60 days of his arrival in Minneapolis, he heard that the Politics Club of Washburn High School had been denied

The Reverend John Cummins' installation (below) included his predecessor, the Reverend Carl Olson (center), and his father, the Reverend Robert Cummins, head of the Universalist Church of America.

the opportunity to hear a lecture by University of Minnesota Professor Mulford Q. Sibley on the virtues and vices of communism. Despite some objections from his trustees, Cummins invited Washburn's entire student body and their parents to hear Sibley speak at First Universalist Church. "I assumed I had every right and, in fact, every obligation on the principles we believe in to be open to all kinds of ideas and encourage youth to think about things," says Cummins. "How could they fight communism if they didn't even know what it was?"

Cummins was a committed civil rights activist and, in 1965, went to Selma, Alabama, to attend the memorial service for the Reverend James Reeb, a northern Unitarian Universalist minister who had been murdered there and to march with Dr. Martin Luther King, Jr., and 600 northern clergy members, 200 of whom were UU ministers. After five days in Selma, Cummins was driven out of town in the middle of the night by a young black man whose acquaintance he had made. "I had to lie down on the floor of the back seat, because the state police told us flat out they couldn't protect us from the vigilantes roaming the highways outside of Selma," he recalled.

In 1978 Cummins was granted an honorary doctorate by Meadville Lombard Theological School at the University of Chicago. In 1991 he and Dru received the Unitarian Universalist Association's Distinguished Service Award. He was an ardent humanist, saying the merger of the Unitarians and Universalists was "a brave experiment in the name of religion," and was especially proud of the 17 women and men he helped to enter the ministry. Cummins served on a number of denominational boards and committees, including 12 years as ministerial settlement representative for the Prairie Star District, of which he was one of the early presidents. He was named Minister Emeritus of First Universalist after his retirement in 1986. Cummins' book of sermons, *This Strange and Wondrous Journey*, was published in 1991.

—*Marie Nordberg*

One of the Reverend John Cummins' first controversial decisions was to invite Professor Mulford Q. Sibley (above) to educate students and their parents about communism.

Cummins ran for the state legislature, served two terms as president of the United Nations Association of Minnesota, and was invited to the White House Conference on International Cooperation by President Lyndon Johnson.

THE REVERENDS SUSAN MILNOR AND TERRY SWEETSER (1988-1995)

The benediction with which the Reverends Susan Milnor and Terry Sweetser closed every service was inspired by the poem "Meditation" by the Reverend Arthur Graham, a mentor of Sweetser's. They substituted the theme of that day's sermon and adapted the words: *"Each of us is a dreamer whose task it is to dream together. It is for today and for times we shall never see, so let us be about the task. The materials are very precious and they are perishable. May it be so."* From 1988 to 1995 co-ministers Milnor and Sweetser kept the congregation "about the task" of welcoming new members, of expanding programming and of planning for the future.

They arrived following a two-year interim period at the close of the Reverend John Cummins' 23-year-ministry. The congregation was excited by the possibilities of a co-ministry and delighted to have both a female and male voice in the pulpit on a regular basis.

Sweetser was a fifth generation Universalist from New England, a graduate of Oberlin College, who received his bachelor of divinity degree from Harvard Divinity School. He came from the Unitarian Universalist Congregation of Atlanta with a reputation as a talented preacher with a gift for fundraising. Sweetser also understood the management aspects of a large church and, as the congregation grew, directed the expansion of the staff and the visioning required to move to larger space. In addition to counseling the Board of Trustees on how to

Installation service of the Reverends Terry Sweetser and Susan Milnor, October 9, 1988

think about the needs of a large church, he knew how to involve every congregant in the process—from standing on the church steps, rain or shine, to greet worshippers before every service to creating dyads and triads of conversation around the need to move from 50th and Girard.

Milnor grew up in Knoxville, Tennessee, and received both her bachelor of arts and master of arts degrees in English literature from the University of Tennessee. She taught at Auburn University for five years, then entered law school at the University of Virginia. But the fit wasn't right, and she left law school for theological school, grasped by the ministry, she said. She received her master of divinity degree in 1986 from Harvard Divinity School and served the Unitarian Universalist Fellowship in Macon, Georgia, before coming to Minnesota.

Ginger Luke, director of religious education during the Sweetser/Milnor ministry, in characterizing their preaching styles, said: "Each of them was a treat. Terry, with his memorized sermons always connecting to UU history in some way. Susan speaking directly to our emotions in the most intellectual way, with words that had a life of their own."

The period of the co-ministry was also a time of swift change and tumultuous events. In 1990 the very premature birth of their daughter Abby, and Milnor's nearly fatal toxemia, rallied the congregation around the family. Church members prepared meals, baked bread and tended to the health of the flowers at the Sweetser/Milnor house. Abby grew and thrived, as did the congregation.

By 1994 a combination of events, including personal challenges and the rapidly changing pressures of the greatly expanded staff and congregation, came to a head. After a difficult period for the lay leadership, the church staff, and the ministers, the co-ministry came to an end. Sweetser preached his last sermon in 1995 and Milnor did the same a few months later. Following their departure, the congregation was blessed with three interim ministers—the Reverends Wayne

Carol Jackson (seated), chair of the Ministerial Search Committee that brought Milnor and Sweetser to First Universalist, recalled that, in a candidate interview, they said it was important for congregants to leave each service with a feeling of hope because no one knew who was suffering at that moment. "They were committed to a ministry of spiritual nurturing and social justice," she said.

You've let us into your lives and welcomed us into yours; you've asked for our stories, listened to our spiritual travels, our fears and hopes. We've shared the confusion and turmoil of war in the Gulf, the riot in Los Angeles, national and international concerns; we've shared the unions and deaths of friends and members, the naming and celebrations of our children; we shared the fear and joy of your daughter's birth—three months early. None of us who were here the Sunday just after Abby was born will forget singing "Happy Birthday, Abigail."

You've helped us know we're in it together, this joyful struggle to live and love and celebrate life in this world and to build an inclusive religious home that welcomes and has room for all people and that will be here for times that we shall never see.

—May 16, 1993, tribute on the fifth anniversary of the co-ministry, by Kathy Coskran, president of the congregation

Robinson, Sheryl Wurl and Ken Brown—to stay the course over the next two years while a new Ministerial Search Committee surveyed the congregation and launched the search for a new settled minister.

—*John Addington with contributions from others*

Susan Milnor and Terry Sweetser with daughter, Abby

UNDER THE CO-MINISTRY TEAM

- *The church hired the denomination's first full-time social justice coordinator, who also served as youth adviser.*

- *The church launched its annual summer service at the Lake Harriet Bandshell.*

- *The annual all-church auction was started.*

- *The social justice coordinator and youth adviser, Bob Knuth, in concert with Sweetser, instituted the Unity Summer program, which provides summer employment at social-service agencies for teens from the church and the community.*

- *Sweetser provided the vision and support for the Universal Mind Bookstore.*

- *Sweetser transferred to First Universalist a sermon-publishing operation, Rising Press, that he had begun in Atlanta, and a volunteer staff published several volumes, including books of sermons by Milnor and John Cummins.*

- *Milnor started the Befrienders program with training by the Wilder Foundation.*

- *Sweetser recommended 4x4 dinners, mixing GLBT and straight people.*

- *Having outgrown the space at 5000 Girard Avenue South, the congregation made the decision to move to 3400 Dupont Avenue South.*

THE REVEREND FRANK RIVAS (1997-2007)

After the departure of the Reverends Terry Sweetser and Susan Milnor, the church needed a particular kind of minister. Laura Cooper, who would become a member of the Reverend Frank Rivas's Committee on Ministry, observed that Rivas's more introverted and reflective personality offered what the church needed most at the time—an ability to emphasize coming together, while respecting differences.

On May 4, 1997, members voted to call Rivas, an openly gay man, then minister of the First Unitarian Universalist Church of Columbus, Ohio, as First Universalist's senior minister. Rivas received his bachelor and master of arts degrees from the University of Illinois, and his master of divinity from Thomas Starr King School for the Ministry. One condition of his accepting the call was the church hiring an associate minister. First Universalist was fortunate that the Reverend Kate Tucker was ready to move to the Twin Cities from Seattle and able to assume that position. Rivas chose the title of Parish Minister, rather than Senior Minister, to reinforce their partnership and his sense of ministering to a community. He felt particularly called to address issues of human rights, especially racism and homophobia.

It was the Reverend Frank Rivas who introduced the Buddhist gong to the worship service and the practice of being called to worship by the sound of the bell.

Rivas' sermons were frequently intellectual and scholarly, challenging the congregation to follow his thought processes as he sought to give contemporary meaning to teachings of Buddhism, stories from the New Testament, contemporary and ancient poetry. Because he preached from an outline in order to be present in the moment with the congregation, his sermons were not available in printed form, but rather in audio recordings.

Church member Kathy Coskran described Rivas as "an empathetic listener who looked for the intrinsic good in people and asked the bigger question. We need to take this deeper, he would say. He used humor gently, to ease a situation or simply to acknowledge the presence of the absurd."

The Reverends Frank Rivas and Kate Tucker (seated center and left), along with executive committee members, dined in 2004 with Unitarian Universalist Association President the Reverend Bill Sinkford (standing center).

In his 10 years of shared ministry, Rivas worked to harmonize the diverse perspectives within his parish. The invasion of Iraq in 2003 was a potentially divisive issue for the congregation. A resolution opposing the anticipated war was brought to a vote at a congregational meeting. The resolution passed by a wide margin, but Rivas encouraged respect for the dissenting voters.

Rivas broadened the role of worship associates, which interim minister the Reverend Ken Brown had created. Under Rivas's leadership, lay worship leaders took on expanded responsibilities for designing and presenting a series of thematic summer Sunday worship services. He also adopted the practice of taking a special outreach collection during services once a month to support an organization in the larger community.

Prior to Rivas' arrival, the board had been researching the adoption of a large-church model of governance. As time went on it was increasingly clear that the size and complexity of church programs, budgets and activities required a strong administrator and assertive leadership. After years of intense lay leader assessment, including exploring various ways of managing decision-making, church leaders reached the conclusion that a different kind of ministerial leadership was required. Rivas agreed to step down in 2006.

It was a difficult period but Rivas managed the transition with grace. His reflective approach was appreciated by many congregants who were saddened by the news of his departure. He preached his last sermon in January 2007, and a farewell reception was held in his honor.

—*John Addington*

1996 Ministerial Search

In 1996 the congregation was surveyed about "what you most hope to get when you attend a service?" The response:
- Inspiration (670, or 86% of respondents)
- Intellectual stimulation (530, or 66%)
- Aesthetic enjoyment (522, or 65%)
- Community (488, or 60%)
- Social justice (205, or 25%)

For the question "what are the most important qualities in a minister?" the response was:
- outstanding spiritual leadership
- intellectual leadership
- organizational facilitation

The Reverend Kate Tucker (1997–   )

We are a community of faith drawn together not by doctrine, but by our desire to be a people of open minds, open hearts, and open hands. We seek to live lives of integrity, in grateful relationship with one another and with that sustaining, transforming power many call God and we often call Love.
—the Reverend Kate Tucker

If you stepped into the sanctuary at First Universalist Church of Minneapolis on a Sunday morning and had trouble finding a seat, it was almost certainly a Reverend-Kate-Tucker-in-the-pulpit Sunday. Her laid-back, friendly demeanor and thoughtful sermons, sprinkled with humor, made her popular with young and old, members and friends alike.

Tucker grew up in Decatur, Illinois. She earned a bachelor of arts in English literature and psychology from Earlham College, a master of fine arts in theater from the University of Minnesota, and master of ministry degree from Earlham School of Religion. She also had a Rockefeller Fellowship year at Southern California School of Theology at Claremont. Tucker was ordained at First Unitarian Church in Portland, Oregon, where she held an interim associate position. She was called by First Universalist Church of Minneapolis as associate minister in September 1998, after serving the previous year on a contract basis. She considers associate ministry to be her special calling.

Tucker and the Reverend Frank Rivas collaborated in many areas of church life. Her ministry at First Universalist focused on spirituality and pastoral care. She led Sunday services approximately monthly, officiated at most memorial services and many weddings, served as pastoral counselor, and supported lay leaders and staff in a variety of ways. She worked with lay pastoral care leaders and the visiting nurse of TRUST—a faith-based community service group in the area—to encourage members to embody their mutual care in specific ways, through listening, the sharing of meals and rides, knitted shawls, messages of support, and more.

"My ministry," Tucker said, "is to see the light in others and name it.

The Reverends Rivas and Tucker truly shared the ministry.

Collaboration is my main mode."

In 1999, Tucker and several lay leaders created Welcome Home Wednesday, an intergenerational midweek evening that included worship, dinner, workshops, and a community closing circle at 9 p.m., which ran for five years. In 2001, Tucker also worked with a group of lay leaders to launch an experiment in small group ministry called Sharing Circles.

During the years after Rivas' departure, Tucker's presence provided the congregation with continuity, or, as she metaphorically called it, fascia tissue. She is an inspiration to many in every area of church life, joining congregants on the lawn of the State Capitol to demonstrate for gay rights, marching down Hennepin Avenue to protest U.S. involvement in Iraq and spending hours at the Minneapolis Convention Center helping the city's less fortunate through Project Homeless Connect.

Tucker has a great sense of humor, loves to dance, and sang with the choir to record a song commissioned for the sesquicentennial celebration.

"How good it is," Tucker said, "to serve a community that prizes transformation, that helps us notice and soften the rigid places inside, that helps us cry real tears over real losses and keep our sense of humor about the rest, that grounds our justice efforts in a sense of wonder and a stance of gratitude."

—*Marie Nordberg*

Tucker watches as the Reverend Laurie Bushbaum creates handmade books for a 1998 summer religious education class.

INTERIM MINISTERS

First Universalist has been fortunate to have been served by capable interim ministers during periods of transition. At the conclusion of the Reverend John Cummins' ministry in 1986, the trustees contracted with the Reverend Brooks Walker to handle the interim ministry duties. Walker was diagnosed with pancreatic cancer and had to withdraw from the position just before he was to begin his duties. On short notice, the church was able to retain the services of the Reverend Ted Webb from Sacramento, California. Webb had recently retired and was in the process of writing a book on the Washburn family; Minneapolis was a good stop for him since the Washburns played a large role in the early days of Minneapolis. When a second year of interim ministry was needed, the trustees contracted with Armida Alexander to serve until 1988. Alexander was a former intern ministry student at First Universalist and completing her seminary work.

Interim ministers at First Universalist who served between the Sweetser/Milnor and Rivas ministries have included: the Reverend Wayne Robinson, a Pentecostal Holiness minister from Oklahoma who found Unitarian Universalism at the age of 53 and served for six months before taking a parish in Fort Myers, Florida; the Reverend Sheryl Wurl, who had been employed at First Universalist for a year as a social action coordinator, was serving as part-time minister at Minnesota Valley UU Fellowship in Bloomington, and became a half-time interim minister, with a focus on adult programming and pastoral care; and the Reverend Ken Brown, who organized Worship Associates to be more inclusive of the congregation during his year.

The Reverend Ted Tollefson served for four months in 2006 when the Reverend Frank Rivas was on sabbatical, and then again in 2007 following Rivas' departure. Tollefson urged the congregation to Wake Up, Stand Up, and Speak Out about peace and justice issues.

The Reverend Charlotte Cowtan (pictured above) served First Universalist as interim minister from 2007 to 2009. She was the church's first specialist in interim ministry. Cowtan helped the board develop policies for the governance handbook and worked with staff to boost morale and create accountability. She facilitated visioning workshops that helped the congregation recognize its strengths and priorities.

According to an article in the UUWorld (Fall 2005), "The role of an interim is to help a congregation make changes between settled ministries, correct problems, and prepare the way for the next minister. The interim is not a juggernaut who comes in and creates change wholesale," said the Reverend John Weston, the UUA's ministerial settlement director. "The interim is more like a mirror, reflecting the congregation back to itself. When the congregation decides on changes it wishes to make, it consults with the minister on how to make them. And the interim points out things the congregation might not see about itself.'"

Church Staff

First Universalist has had some long ministries, but even longer service has been given by church staff, primarily female office administrators, called secretaries in the early days. Marion Griffith was only 18 years old when she began working at Church of the Redeemer under the tutelage of Evelyn Hughes, who worked as the church secretary for 44 years. Griffith's church career lasted 37 years. She trained her successor, Clarice (Claire) Burk, who put in 29 years at the church office. In all, these three women served the church for 110 years.

"You must have heard a lot of sermons," the Reverend John Cummins said to Marion Griffith (above). "No," Griffith replied, "they only have about three. They just say it in different ways."

Marion Griffith assisted the Reverend Marion Shutter until his death in 1939, then worked with the Reverend Carl Olson, and, at the end of her career, the Reverend John Cummins. She was active with youth, served as historian for the church and Unity House, was a substitute religious education director and Sunday school teacher, a Girl Scout leader, and volunteered for the Association of Universalist Women. Whether a committee was in trouble or a family in need, she was quick to respond with a ready ear, efficient hand, and compassionate heart. Some called her a minister to the ministers. During his later days, Shutter's health was poor and he preached from a chair. So that he didn't have to stand for long periods of time, Griffith greeted the congregants for him. She retired in 1964 but played an active role in the church and AUW through 1992.

Before retiring in 1964, Griffith trained **Claire Burk** (below) as office assistant. Claire was in her late 20s when she started working at the church. For most of her 29-year tenure, she worked alone and did everything: answered the phones, typed the sermons, edited and mailed the *Liberal* newsletter. Burk went about her work deliberately, and worked well into the evening when necessary. She and her family lived near the church, so she was available to her three daughters when they needed her and the church benefited by their occasional assistance in the office.

By 1984 the complexities of church management made it clear that the church needed a bookkeeper in addition to a secretary. Burk trained **Sharon**

Moving Forward: 1939-2009 51

Maciej (right) in First Universalist procedures and the two made up the office staff for several years. Maciej had worked as an assistant controller for Jostens for 12 years and also with the Savage State Bank, so arrived with ample financial experience. Cummins called her *Sharon Magic*. Maciej gained insight into members' difficulties through her work and was soon drawn into a pastoral care role. She sometimes bought and delivered food to members, and once even delivered food to a member's cat. Maciej's flexibility served her well as she worked through several ministerial transitions involving five settled ministers and six interim ministers.

The congregation grew rapidly in the early years of the Milnor/Sweetser co-ministry, as did the church staff. Finding the right balance between tasks to be accomplished and financial resources to support growing staff needs, was challenging. By 2009, the staff had grown to include a director of administration, director of congregational life, director of faith in action, facility coordinator/financial assistant, membership support coordinator, children's program coordinator, youth and young adult ministries coordinator, program assistant/childcare coordinator, and communications coordinator.

—*Mary Junge*

Claire Burk formed the Liberal Folding Group, a group of retired church members who volunteered twice a month to prepare the Liberal for mailing. Co-hort Sharon Maciej formalized the popular volunteer job which was a source of fellowship as well as productivity for the members who came. Pictured left: Don Wilson, Mary Djerf, office manager Mary Ann Dean, Marge Bielke.

MEMBERS MILDRED OLSON AND GRACE WILSON

Grace Wilson (left) and Mildred Olson on October 9, 1988, installation Sunday for the Reverends Susan Milnor and Terry Sweetser.

Along with the Reverend John Cummins, Mildred Olson was instrumental in starting the Carl and Mildred Olson Ministerial Education Fund, which by 2009 had assisted 27 students and interns in entering the liberal ministry—a cherished legacy.

Mildred Boone Olson served First Universalist Church in many capacities along with her husband, the Reverend Carl Olson. She shared credit with him in rebuilding the membership after the severe decline in the pre-war years.

Mildred Boone was born in 1905 and raised in the Universalist church in Muncie, Indiana. As a young woman she attended national conventions of the Young People's Christian Union where she met her future husband. They were married in 1930. At each church in which Olson served, she was his tactful, friendly right hand. At his invitation, she was also a careful critic of his sermons.

One of the challenges facing the church when the Olsons arrived in 1939 was the existence of two similar but competing women's associations, the Ladies Social Circle and the Women's Association, then known as the Association of Universalist Women (AUW). Mrs. Olson was an effective facilitator and brought the two groups together as one.

Olson remained active in church affairs after her husband's death in 1965, serving on the AUW Board and as chair of the Friendship Committee.

Grace Scofield Wilson was born in Minneapolis in 1909 and was baptized at the Tuttle Church of Minneapolis. She met her husband, Harold Wilson, at the youth group there. She completed college in 1939 in home economics and later took writing courses. While raising her children, Wilson volunteered in a political party, the Foreign Policy Association, Parent-Teacher Association, scouts, and for the League of Women Voters, where she was employed in 1950. In addition to her work with AUW, Wilson served on the church Board of Trustees, was a delegate to the national church convention, attended training sessions at the Universalist Camp on Lake Michigan, sang in the choir, chaired committees to help people in trouble, and formed the Rainbow Club to enhance awareness about racial issues.

—information from
100 Years of Liberation: Association of Universalist Women: Minneapolis 1905-2005

Excerpt from "To Have and to Hold: The Story of a Marriage," by Grace Scofield Wilson, 1988

After 33 years of marriage, Grace Wilson's husband, Harold, suffered a brain aneurysm in 1963 and spent 22 years in a nursing home. She wrote a book about her experiences and successfully advocated for legislation to regulate nursing homes. In May 1979, the Wilsons filed a class action suit about medical assistance. Because she could not afford his nursing home costs, Wilson announced that they would divorce so that her husband would qualify for medical assistance and they might avoid poverty. The judge ruled in the Wilson's favor, and they remained married. The State Legislature revised the eligibility requirements for medical assistance. Wilson declared one of her greatest triumphs to be her role in getting new legislation passed to revise eligibility requirements for medical assistance in 1979.

While Harold and I awaited the judge's decision concerning the availability of a spouse's funds to pay nursing home costs, I started on a project with the Nursing Home Residents Advisory Council. . . . We voted to call ourselves Friends and Relatives of Nursing Home Residents. We started a newsletter. We set up a series of meetings to educate ourselves. . . . The council staff helped us understand government's role in nursing home matters. They explained that the Minnesota Legislature was starting its session in early January, and the Council was planning to support several bills, one of which was to change eligibility requirements for Medical Assistance. . . . My friends said, "You are just the type we need to make a persuasive, informed argument."

When the day came, I was chauffeured by friends to the Capitol in St. Paul. A young staff member, who treated me as a valuable resource, took my arm to steer me safely across the busy street. Pretty heady stuff! And yet in a way I felt insulted. "I'm not that old," I said to myself. When we reached the hearing room, I noted the huge oak table with the Chairman of the Senate Health and Welfare Committee seated at the head. Around the sides in arm chairs were about 20 senators, mostly men, a few women. Quite a group to confront. . . . Several persons spoke before I did. When it was my turn I got up, held my notes tightly in my hand, cleared my throat, and reminded myself that it was not *me* but the message that was important. So I spoke slowly, with emphasis and loud enough for those in the back row to hear.

I told them frankly and in detail about Harold's and my experience, and ended with, "I think it's immoral and rotten for my government to put me in the position of having to consider divorce in order to avoid poverty for myself." I asked their support of revisions to the law, which would raise the assets limitation from $1,000 to $15,000, the cash-in value of insurance from $1,000 to $10,000, and would exempt the house and car from consideration. We were delighted when our bill passed that committee unanimously.

The bill was later passed out of several more committees, voted on by the full Senate and House, and finally signed into law by the Governor.

MAKING A DIFFERENCE IN THE DENOMINATION

When the American Unitarian Association and the Universalist Church of America consolidated in 1961, a new organization was born—the Unitarian Universalist Association (UUA), an association of congregations. Aspects from both denominations were incorporated in forming this new entity. This non-hierarchical denomination retained one very important contribution from the Universalists—an open, transparent government.

The members of the UUA are local, self-governing congregations, loosely organized into a number of geographic districts. The UUA Board of Trustees are either elected by each one of the UUA's 20 districts or are elected at large by the delegates attending the annual General Assembly. Resolutions are also adopted at General Assembly urging Unitarian Universalist congregations to support both religious and political actions. As a result of this democratic organization, lay people as well as ministers are encouraged, appointed or elected to engage in the governance and activities of the UUA.

Why be active in the denomination? There are many possible answers. A larger group not only wields more influence, but makes it easier for like-minded seekers to find a Unitarian Universalist church wherever they are. It makes it possible to draw on the collective wisdom and legacy of others who believe in the Universalist message of love and hope. The denomination is a touchstone for all member congregations, large and small: a source of inspiration and principles and a way to make our voice heard beyond our own street, neighborhood, city, or state.

So there are global reasons to make sure the denomination is effective, but there are also personal ones. First Universalist members who have represented the church at the annual General Assembly speak of the power of being one among many. They return enthusiastic, brimming with new ideas, as any convention-goer does, but it is the power of the Service of the Living Tradition with hundreds of other Unitarian Universalists that stays with them. Participation in the denomination matters.
And First Universalists have certainly participated over the ages.

From the very beginning, members of First Universalist Church of Minneapolis have been represented at the denominational level.

First Universalist Church's the Reverend Meg Riley (above) served the UUA most recently as director of Advocacy and Witness Programs. The Reverend Harlan Limpert (below) served most recently as the UUA's vice president for Ministries and Congregational Support.

William D. Washburn served as president of the Universalist Church of America. Since the merger in 1961, members of First Universalist have been active and influential in the denomination, both at the UUA headquarters in Boston, in the Prairie Star District (PSD) and in the Twin Cities area.

The Reverend John Cummins, shortly after his arrival in Minnesota, became the president of PSD, served the district for several years as ministerial settlement representative, and for a while, the PSD offices were housed in the Girard church. As noted elsewhere, Drusilla Cummins was extremely active at the regional and national level in many areas. Both of them were honored by the UUA with the Distinguished Service Award.

Another indication of the level of denominational commitment of First Universalists is the list of honorees at the denominational level. The church was recognized by both the UUA and PSD with the O. Eugene Pickett Awards in 1993 for outstanding contributions to the growth of Unitarian Universalism. Other PSD award recipients from the congregation included: Frances Howard, Unsung UU Award in 1988; the Reverend Meg Riley, Ellie Morton Award in 1989; Ginger Luke, Ellie Morton Award in 1990; Abby Washburn, Youth Social Justice Award in 1994; Carol Jackson, Unsung UU Award in 1996, the President's Award in 2003, and the Betty Gorshe Heritage Award in 2009; Nancy Atchison, Keeping the Faith Award in 2001; Katie Sullivan, Youth Social Justice Award in 2001; Barbara Kellett, the President's Award in 2005; Tom Atchison, the Adult Social Justice Award in 2003.

The multiple levels of denominational involvement of those First Universalists and more than 30 others is broad and deep. Members have chaired UUA and PSD committees, planned conferences, advised on social justice issues and worked with bylaws and compensation. In 1967, First Universalist assisted the creation of the Minnesota Valley Unitarian Universalist Fellowship. The legacy of involvement at the local, regional, and national level has been both a source of pride for First Universalists and a reminder of the responsibility to look beyond the congregation in spreading the Universalist message.
—*Carol Jackson, Kathy Coskran and Nancy Atchison*

Honored First Universalists have included (top to bottom) Ginger Luke, Nancy Atchison and Carol Jackson.

Church Homes

Church House, at 4600 Dupont Avenue South, became the church home in 1941.

The cornerstone-laying ceremony for the new church finally got underway in 1948.

4600 Dupont Avenue South

When the congregation sold the large Church of the Redeemer building in downtown Minneapolis to the Catholic Archdiocese in 1941 for $112,500 (per an acceptance letter from then-board president Alfred Pillsbury), the plan was to build a smaller structure immediately, in a space more accessible to the congregation, which was moving farther south. But with the intervention of war, building materials could not be spared for the development of a church.

Although cramped for many years into the three-story Church House, it was perhaps a blessing in disguise, in more ways than one. According to Mildred Olson, wife of the Reverend Carl Olson, long-time board president Pillsbury was "a very shy man" who often stood alone at the downtown church, but got better acquainted with people at the Church House. "We sat so close together we had to get to know each other."

The first floor was for the sanctuary, five bedrooms on second floor were used as classrooms, and an assembly room was on the third.

It wasn't until May 23, 1948, that the cornerstone was laid for a new church at 5000 Girard Avenue South. As Olson said in a sermon, "Handicaps often provide strength. So it has been for us. We have been crowded here in our Church House, but it has made us closer friends, both figuratively and literally. . . . We have relinquished many of the things which we had come to accept as a matter of course, but we shall appreciate them the more when we are able to have them again."

By the time the new building was dedicated in 1949, the congregation had grown under Olson, and was ready for the pleasures and challenges of its new space.

Moving Forward: 1939-2009

5000 Girard Avenue South

The 18,000-square-foot red brick building at the corner of 50th Street and Girard Avenue South was reminiscent of the New England churches of the Universalist heritage. In the beginning, the sanctuary had pews and a baptismal font that the Reverend James Tuttle had acquired for the church nearly 100 years earlier, when baptism was a Universalist ritual. After a major remodeling, the pews and the font were removed and new classroom space was acquired.

In 1975, a typical year, the church housed public forums, Thursday chess club, Friday bridge club, the Universalist blood bank, a nursery school, youth and singles groups, Al-Anon, denominational meetings, more than 20 church committees, and potluck groups centered around parenting, marriage, theater, camping, cooking, reading, music and photography.

After nearly 40 years in the Girard space, the rapid growth of the congregation brought a capacity crisis. In 1968, a Site and Size Committee was formed to discuss finding solutions for housing 587 members and 414 registered Sunday School children in a building designed for no more than 500 people. Initially it was decided to stay in the space, rent school space, and move to two Sunday morning services. But after the congregation grew so much that three services were needed, a Buildings Committee was formed in 1990 to consider options.

After nearly two years of searching, including looking at properties in the suburbs, it was learned that the 44,000-square-foot Adath Jeshurun Synagogue in the Uptown area of Minneapolis was selling its building and moving to Minnetonka. The space offered seating for 900 and much more space for classrooms. After raising $1.5 million, the congregation purchased the building and marched from 5000 Girard to 3400 Dupont Avenue South on July 25, 1993.

We have witnessed many changes in the church over the years . . . The remodeling project, which did away with the traditional church arrangement of pews, caused consternation among many members. But the majority agreed that the new seating arrangement was more flexible and seemed to provide a warmer, welcoming atmosphere.
—Jim and Janet Chandler, 1992

The early days of 50th and Girard (left), with pews, gave way to a makeover with chairs (right) to provide more flexibility.

Packing and Walking

From 1949 to 1993, services were held at 5000 Girard Avenue South until the congregation outgrew its capacity. On July 25, 1993, a group was pictured at the Girard building (top) before its procession to 3400 Dupont Avenue South (below).

MOVING FORWARD: PROCESSION ARRIVES AT DUPONT CHURCH

Moving Forward: 1939-2009

3400 Dupont Avenue South

Making a lovely old synagogue feel like a Universalist church was both a financial issue and a creative opportunity. The congregation didn't want to lose the character of the old building, but also needed to make it feel like home. The painted glass windows depicting scenes of Jewish history and holidays were a particular challenge. After an extensive search for groups that might be interested, the windows were salvaged by the Gaytee Stained Glass studio of Minneapolis—one is now housed at the Minneapolis Institute for Arts—and replaced with clear glass that floods the sanctuary with daylight.

Above: the service of dedication October 24, 1993, before the original synagogue window glass was removed. Below: The first Sunday at the new church home, July 25, 1993.

Other remodeling included changes to the chancel, remodeling a storage space into a spacious library, replacing solid wooden entrance doors with glass ones, constructing the atrium to illumine the space between the main building (of 1927) and education wing (of 1953), replacing outdated carpet, installing a permanent labyrinth in the social hall, and creating a chapel for small services, dedicated as the Cummins Room in 1997.

—*Mikki Morrissette with contributions from John Addington*

Buildings and Grounds

"Our household of faith shows forth our liberal beliefs: large windows that let in the natural light of day and do not shut us off from life, an open room for the sharing of our dreams, the dissipation of our loneliness, and the encouragement of our public and private struggles. It is possible because each of us believes it to be an affirmation of something beautiful, and each does what he or she can."
—the Reverend John Cummins

Thanks to the gentle prodding of Evelyn Prestemon, an outdoor beautification project took root at 5000 Girard in 1978 when 25 trees were planted on the church grounds. The following year, 16 volunteers planted more trees, shrubs and bulbs. As the Reverend John Cummins reported, Prestemon and her team planted, Dan Bishop and his sons laid concrete steps, Bob Oswood crafted new tiles, and Chuck Thiele was "digging around the roots of elms on what was supposed to be a vacation."

After relocating to 3400 Dupont, the Buildings and Grounds (BAG) Committee took on the task of improving the new space. In 1996, a team found ways to implement energy saving steps in the sanctuary, checked insulation issues, organized an infrared heat scan to assess potential heat loss in the ceiling, and anticipated window glazing and painting projects.

Buildings and grounds work has long involved Dan Bishop (top). The landscaping crew of Evelyn Prestemon, June Blanchard, Inger Palm and Lisa Heinrich (above). The Mary E. Carter Library at 5000 Girard (right).

Library

The library has long been an important amenity of church life. Mary E. Carter was one who gave many hours to its care. Don Carter donated money to pay for comfortable leather reading chairs and other furniture. To honor them, the library was named the Mary E. Carter Library. The Library Committee helped First Universalist Church embrace its second 150 years by updating the library with Internet access and a revamping of its book collection.

THIS WE BELIEVE

We, the member congregations of the Unitarian Universalist Association, covenant to affirm and promote:

The inherent worth and dignity of every person;
Justice, equity and compassion in human relations;
Acceptance of one another and encouragement to spiritual growth in our congregations;
A free and responsible search for truth and meaning;
The right of conscience and the use of the democratic process within our congregations and in society at large;
The goal of world community with peace, liberty, and justice for all;
Respect for the interdependent web of all existence of which we are a part.

—adopted by the Unitarian Universalist Association in 1985

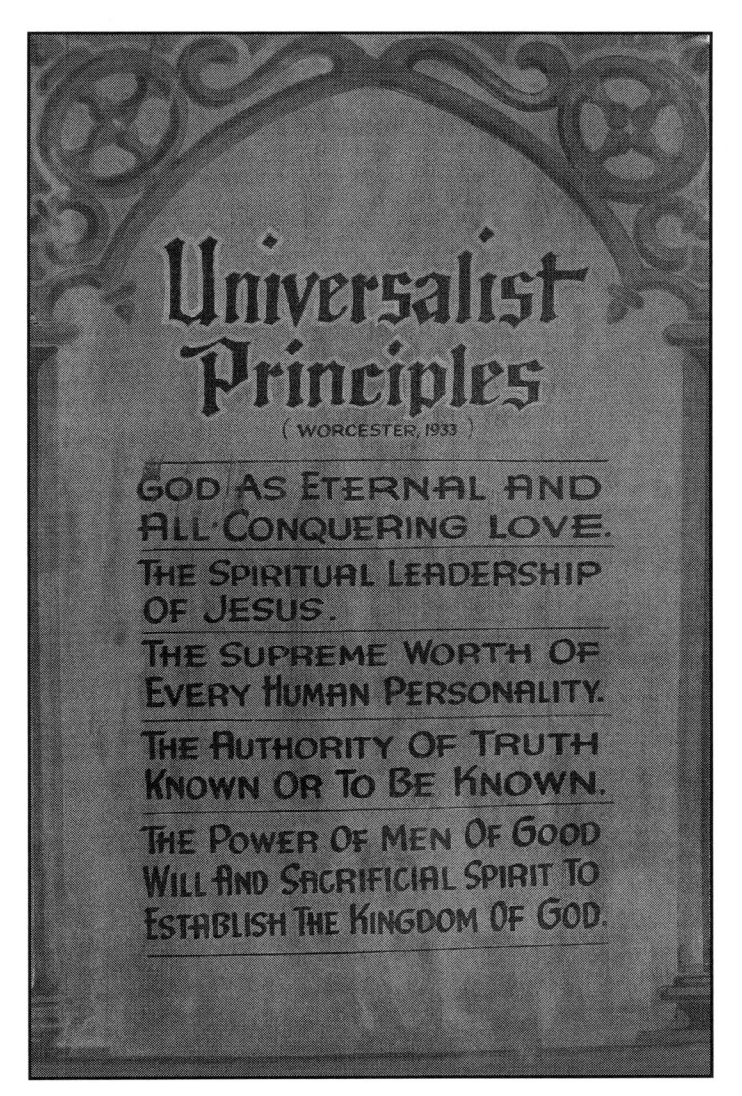

The Church of the Redeemer owned this large poster of the Bond of Faith, the principles adopted by the Universalists of the day. It was left behind when the congregation moved from Church House at 4600 Dupont Avenue. In 1990, Karin Wille, president of the congregation, met the current owner of the house through business. After they discovered the First Universalist connection, he excitedly retrieved this poster to return to the church. He had nearly thrown it away several times, he said, but hadn't. "Any church which held these beliefs couldn't be all bad," he added.

LOVE IS THE DOCTRINE OF THIS CHURCH

Love is the doctrine of this church
The quest for truth its sacrament
And service is its prayer.
To dwell together in peace
To serve humanity in fellowship
To the end that all persons
shall grow in harmony with themselves and each other.
This is our agreement as free persons in a free religious community.

It has long been challenging to summarize what Universalists and, later, Unitarian Universalists believe. The Reverend Terry Sweetser encouraged congregants to create an elevator speech—what one would say in a minute or two to describe what UUs believe. Belief statements could be more specific in 1859 when our founders and early ministers held a loose belief in the Trinity, or at least the spiritual importance of Jesus.

Theirs was a liberal and inclusive Christianity, set apart from other denominations by its foundation of universal salvation. As time went on, the distinction blurred between First Universalist and other local churches as the concept of God in other denominations became more loving. As explained in the article that follows, from the early nineteenth century, the Universalists worked to articulate their beliefs without creating a creed. This struggle resulted in the Universalists revisiting and revising their faith statement in 1803, 1870, 1899 and 1935. When the Universalists united with the Unitarians in 1961, the denomination had a set of purposes and principles adopted in 1959 that was revised in 1985.

The Reverend John Cummins described his ministerial role as a helper and companion. One of the ways he helped was by providing words that the congregation repeated every Sunday for more than two decades, the words written above that became the church's implicit creed.

One UU minister observed that the most recent statement of principles is "an affirmation of the least that UUs hold in common, across the theological and philosophical spectrum." It turns out that "the least" is quite a lot.

This section, *This We Believe,* traces the evolution of those statements of belief and affirmation through what we do—our ceremonies, rites of passage and practices—and what we say from the pulpit—words from our ministers.

The Faith Tradition of Universalism

John Murray, often referred to as the father of American Universalism, arrived on the shores of New Jersey from England in 1770. He was fleeing from a life of tragedy, including the deaths of his wife and child, but he came to the New World with the good news of universal salvation. "Give them, not hell," Murray said, "but hope and courage. Do not push them deeper into their theological despair, but preach the kindness and everlasting love of God."

This message stood in sharp contrast to the predominant Calvinism of the day: that theology held that only those selected by God could be saved, and that good works would not insure salvation. Thirty-three years after Murray preached his first Universalist sermon in the New World, in 1803, the New England Convention of Universalists adopted a three-part Profession of Belief, which came to be known as the **Winchester Profession**. It said:

We believe that the Holy Scriptures of the Old and New Testament contain a revelation of the character of God, and of the duty, interest and final destination of mankind.

We believe there is one God, whose nature is Love, revealed in one Lord Jesus Christ, by one Holy Spirit of Grace, who will finally restore the whole family of mankind to holiness and happiness.

We believe that holiness and true happiness are inseparably connected, and that believers ought to be careful to maintain order, and practice good works, for these things are good and profitable unto men.

The **Winchester Profession** also contained what became known as the **Liberty Clause**. It stated that the churches and societies could adopt articles of faith suited to their particular circumstances, "provided they do not disagree with our general Profession." Although this clause was invoked over the years as guaranteeing freedom of conscience, the quoted phrase makes it clear that liberty of belief was limited.

Major William D. Hale, speaking at the 50th anniversary celebration about the bells of the Church of the Redeemer—"how inspiring their songs of hope and faith, how cordial their welcome"—offered this slightly altered version of the poem "The Creed of the Bells":

*Not faith alone,
but works as well
Must test the soul,
proclaims our bell.
Come here and
cast aside your load
And work your way
along the road,
With faith in God
and faith in man,
And hope in Christ
where hope began.
Do well! Do well!
Do well! Do well!
Peals forth
the Universalist bell.*

The men who met to create the First Universalist Society of Minneapolis on October 24, 1859, were from the East and would have been familiar with Universalist theology. Originally founded as an unincorporated religious association, the preamble to the one page 1859 society constitution stated that the undersigned founders, "being desirous of promoting the cause of liberal Christianity in this community, hereby unite for that purpose."

In 1864 the society incorporated and adopted a new constitution. The purpose of the church, as agreed to by its members, was set forth clearly in the following preamble:

We the subscribers feeling desirous "to grow in grace, and in the knowledge of our Lord and Savior Jesus Christ" do hereby form ourselves into a Society, that we may be helps to each other, and that by our united energies we may better serve the purposes of religion and truth.

Growing in grace, helping each other, and working together to serve religion and truth are still part of First Universalist's theology 145 years later.

Subsequent articles of the new constitution expanded on the founders' original commitment to "liberal Christianity." Article VIII provided that "The Christian Ordinances of Baptism and the Lord's Supper may be regularly administered to this Society as a Church of Christ." Unlike traditional Christian churches, however, the article went on to state that the observance (or non-observance) of the ordinances would be "left to the conscience of each member to decide for himself or herself."

Article X left no doubt about what members of First Universalist believed, as it read "Finally, we adopt as the basis of our religious belief . . ." language which is identical to the Winchester Profession, with one important exception: the Liberty Clause is nowhere to be found. The belief in "one God, whose nature is love, revealed in one Lord Jesus Christ, by one Holy Spirit of Grace," coupled with the commitment to "practice good works," would remain the belief statement of First Universalist for the next 88 years.

In 1870, the Universalists gathered in Gloucester, Massachusetts, to celebrate the 100th anniversary of John Murray's landing in America.

The delegates to the General Convention of the Universalist Church of America adopted a new national constitution that incorporated the Winchester Profession but—consistent with the position of the First Universalist Society—excluded the Liberty Clause. In addition, for the first time, assent to the profession was made a specific requirement for ministerial fellowship.

As the century came to a close, the Universalist denomination continued to struggle with articulating a belief statement that was not a creed. In 1899, following many committee recommendations and years of debate, delegates to the General Convention met in Boston and amended the national constitution to include, again, the Liberty Clause. The requirements for fellowshipping ministers were stated as "the acceptance of the essential principles of the Universalist faith," which included, among other things:

- the Universal Fatherhood of God;
- the spiritual authority and leadership of His Son, Jesus Christ;
- the trustworthiness of the Bible as containing a revelation from God.

The essence of the Liberty Clause reappeared in a statement that no precise forms of words were required as a condition of fellowship, as long as the essential principles were professed. This compromise, known as the Boston Declaration, seemed to satisfy many in the denomination. First Universalist, however, continued to adhere to the Winchester Profession.

By the early twentieth century the theology of so many Protestant denominations had moved toward a God of love that Universalism struggled with whether or not it had become a victim of its own success. This soul searching culminated in a new statement of faith adopted in 1935, called the **Bond of Fellowship**. It was influenced by the social gospel movement and the theology of the Reverend Clarence Skinner, who was a great advocate for making social justice an integral part of the Universalist faith.

The Bond of Fellowship's stated common purpose was "to do the will of God as Jesus revealed it and to cooperate in establishing the kingdom for which he lived and died." To that end Universalists pledged their faith:

All types of Christians now believe in the love of God rather than his hate and believe that the race was benignly created to be the object of love of an Infinite Being rather than for eternal punishment.

—William D. Washburn, presiding officer at the 50th anniversary celebration

". . . in God as Eternal and All Conquering Love, in the spiritual leadership of Jesus, in the supreme worth of every personality, in the authority of truth known or to be known, and in the power of men of goodwill and sacrificial spirit to overcome evil and progressively establish the kingdom of God."

The Liberty Clause appeared as follows: "Neither this nor any other statement shall be imposed as a creedal test, provided always that the principles above stated be professed."

The language of the Bond of Fellowship was a reflection of the times for Universalists, including the impact of the Great Depression, overtures from the Unitarians about combining the two denominations, and the publication of the Humanist Manifesto in 1933. As Charles Howe notes in his book *The Larger Faith: A Short History of American Universalism*, "the changes [in the Bond of Fellowship] from the 1899 declaration are obvious: there is no mention of the Bible, Jesus is no longer referred to as Christ, the doctrine of universal salvation is referred to only obliquely . . . and there is a strong emphasis on the Social Gospel, as evidenced by the statement twice calling for the establishment of the Kingdom of God, in part, at least, through human effort."

As noted earlier, First Universalist was unmoved by the denominational tussles that produced the Boston Declaration and the Bond of Fellowship, preferring to retain the Winchester Profession as its congregational belief statement. In 1952, three years after the congregation dedicated its new home at 5000 Girard Avenue South, the constitution was restated as articles of incorporation and the name was officially changed to the First Universalist *Church* of Minneapolis. The new articles of incorporation replaced the Winchester Profession with the Bond of Fellowship as the stated purpose of the church. This time, the Liberty Clause was included, with language that "neither this nor any other statement shall be imposed as a creedal test."

In 1961 the Universalists and the Unitarians merged to become the Unitarian Universalist Association (UUA), ending at some level the Universalist denominational struggles with creed. Two years earlier the following principles were adopted by UUA members:

What brings us together are the deep and profound questions of life and death, the issues of ultimate good and ultimate meaning, the nature of divinity and of humankind. Essentially, we come together to worship, to achieve a more just world and to be in fellowship.

However much we squabble about the meaning of words, we are a people who yearn for experience and song, language and silence that bring the heart into union with the mind. We know that as useful as science and psychology are, they do not suggest the mystery. The language of religion is the language of the heart, and we long for the heart to speak and be spoken to.

—the Reverend Susan Milnor, in her 1989 sermon "What Do I Say?"

In accordance with these corporate purposes, the members of the Unitarian Universalist Association, dedicated to the principles of a free faith, unite in seeking:

to strengthen one another in a free and disciplined search for truth as the foundation of our religious fellowship;
to cherish and spread the universal truths taught by the great prophets and teachers of humanity in every age and tradition, immemorially summarized in the Judeo-Christian heritage as love to God and love to man;
to affirm, defend and promote the supreme worth of every human personality, the dignity of man, and the use of the democratic method in human relationships;
to implement our vision of one world by striving for a world community founded on ideals of brotherhood, justice and peace;
to serve the needs of member churches and fellowships, to organize new churches and fellowships, and to extend and strengthen liberal religion;
to encourage cooperation with men of goodwill in every land.

Vestiges of the Universalist Bond of Fellowship appear in the principles in the phrases "love to God," "search for truth," and "the supreme worth of every personality." The commitment to establish the kingdom of God on earth reemerged as "striving for a world community founded on ideals of brotherhood, justice and peace."

First Universalist's articles of incorporation were amended again three years later, in 1964, to incorporate the first four principles as the stated purpose of the church. To that was added a statement that "Neither this nor any other statement shall be imposed as a creedal test."

In 1975 the principles in First Universalist's articles of incorporation were amended slightly to eliminate gender bias in the language. The word "man" in the second principle was changed to "humanity." In the third principle, the phrase "the dignity of man" was deleted, and the words "and dignity" were added after the phrase "supreme worth."

In 1985 the delegates to the UUA General Assembly adopted a revision of the 1959 principles. The revised version, still in use in 2009, states:

We, the member congregations of the Unitarian Universalist Association, covenant to affirm and promote:
The inherent worth and dignity of every person;

As we grow older and wiser, we do not reject our parents, Santa Claus, God, Creeds or the Bible. We simply try to understand them better. The liberating church is set up to help [us] do just that ... Out of the elements of all past experience, out of questioning, out of looking at old assumptions in new ways, and in the company of like-minded seekers, we build, by degrees, a religion that is truly our own.
—the Reverend John Cummins, in his sermon "A Religion of Your Own"

Justice, equity and compassion in human relations;
Acceptance of one another and encouragement to spiritual growth in our congregations;
A free and responsible search for truth and meaning;
The right of conscience and the use of the democratic process within our congregations and in society at large;
The goal of world community with peace, liberty and justice for all;
Respect for the interdependent web of all existence of which we are a part.

In 1986, the articles of incorporation for First Universalist were amended again to provide that the purpose of the church, in accordance with the principles of the UUA, shall be to "affirm and promote" the UUA Principles. The language from the 1964 articles that neither this nor any other statement shall be a creedal test was retained.

It bears emphasizing that for the Universalists the 1803 Winchester Profession, the 1899 Boston Declaration and the 1935 Bond of Fellowship are what their language implies—statements of faith, albeit non-creedal ones. Each clause of the Winchester Profession begins "We believe." The Bond of Fellowship states "we avow our faith in . . ." These professions—God as love, Jesus as spiritual authority, the importance of good works—constituted First Universalist's statement of belief for 100 years, from 1864 until 1964. It was not until three years after the merger of the Unitarians and Universalists in 1961 that the purpose of the church shifted from these beliefs to a statement of principles the congregation would affirm and promote.

For much of the church's history, ministers at First Universalist have preached that each and every religious liberal has a moral obligation to examine and build a personal faith—a religion that is truly our own, to quote the Reverend John Cummins—in the company of like-minded seekers. The faith tradition of Universalism is the heritage of the members of First Universalist Church.

—*Karin L. Wille*

Much of the information in this article was taken from *The Larger Faith: A Short History of American Universalism,* by Charles A. Howe, and the Reverend Elizabeth Strong's paper "Are You a Closet Universalist?"

THIS WE BELIEVE: CONGREGATIONAL LIFE

Dancing around the Maypole on Flower Communion Sunday at 5000 Girard Avenue South

First Universalist's legacy of congregational polity is long and deep. The church was created by a small group of Universalists—lay people, not ministers—who founded a church on the west side of the Mississippi River. A layman, William D. Washburn, served on the Board of Trustees for 50 years, through three ministers. By the time the Universalists joined with the Unitarians in 1961, the congregation was not only calling its ministers, but ordaining and installing them.

First Universalist has been blessed with inspired ministerial leadership, but the democratic inclusiveness of Universalist theology means that what we believe is also articulated by how we provide religious education for children, by how we embrace and welcome new members, by the music we perform together, by the art we create, and by the rites of passage and rituals of celebration we create.

Over the years communal spiritual practices beyond the Sunday morning service grew and expanded: some were small, intimate gatherings; others not only included the congregation but regularly attracted people from outside the church community.

We, the people, are the church.

> *We believe that the quest for meaning and understanding is a lifelong process. . . . A written creed implies that the search is over, that your mind and heart and experiences are irrelevant. Thus each Unitarian Universalist is on his or her unique path—yet we walk our paths in community. We learn from each other, not only from our ministers.*
> —Paul Riedesel, member, in "What Do Unitarian Universalists Believe? Some Common Threads," on the First Universalist Church website

Rites of Passage, Rituals of Celebration, Congregational Practices

We dedicate these children to the highest and best of life, to the freedom and discipline of this community, to the great quest for the mystery that lies in their own hearts.

We dedicate ourselves to making this church a place of spiritual growth for children. We dedicate ourselves to making the world a place fit for children. We embark now on that journey together.

Children, we welcome you into this world and into this community. In your names may all of us find joy. By your worth may generations to come be blessed.
—Litany of Dedication, 1994

Weddings and funerals, baptisms and child dedications, teas and holiday celebrations have always been a part of First Universalist Church. In the early days those rites and rituals were similar to the practices found in other denominations.

Children's Dedications

Children's Day was started in June 1856 by the Reverend Charles Hall Leonard, pastor of the Universalist church in Chelsea, Massachusetts. He instituted the practice of public christening at the annual Children's Day service. Earlier, Universalists had rejected the practice due to its association with the idea of being born into original sin, wanting instead an open avowal that our children are God's children, accepted as a sacred trust to be reared "in the nurture and admonition of the Lord."

Children at Church of the Redeemer were christened until the Reverend Carl Olson discontinued the practice in favor of the rose ceremony, in which children were gently tapped with a rose and touched with water. The Reverend John Cummins expanded the focus of the dedication of children to emphasize what adults should do to create a better world for children. The child dedication service continued to evolve but continued with the benediction of the rose with the thorns removed to emphasize the congregation's responsibility for protecting and nurturing children.

Flower Communion

By the late 1960s the congregation was exploring and adopting other communal rituals and practices, some of which continued to embrace aspects of the Universalist Judeo-Christian heritage and others that went beyond that source. The yearning for ritual was perhaps aroused by the turmoil of the times, the national and international cultural shifts, and the empowerment of women. During Cummins' ministry, the congregation began celebrating the Flower Communion created by the Reverend Dr. Norbert Capek of Czechoslovakia in 1923. For many years the older elementary girls at First Universalist danced around the maypole, and everybody brought a flower and took home a different one, an acknowledgement of the interconnectedness of all life. The flowers represented each person, unique and free, joining together in fellowship

"Anyone who wishes to light a candle to acknowledge concern, loss or celebration is invited to do so in the foyer of the Sanctuary before the service."

April 25, 1993
Girard Church

Flower Communion at Lake Harriet Bandshell, 1991

and accepting the other regardless of differences.

Holy Days

In the mid-1980s the congregation began to observe All Souls Day on the Sunday closest to the first of November as a day of remembrance. During the service anyone present could name a loved one who had died recently or in years past. At about that time the church also added a late evening candlelit service on Christmas Eve as a time to step out of the clamor of the commercial aspects of the season and, together, to find a moment of inner quiet. In the early 1990s congregants were invited to light a candle to acknowledge concern, loss or celebration in the foyer of the sanctuary before the Sunday morning service.

Under Northern Skies Women's Ritual Circle

Begun in the mid 1980s by Sharon Bishop and other women, the Under Northern Skies Women's Ritual Circle was a direct outcome of the "Cakes for the Queen of Heaven" curriculum, developed in 1986 by the Unitarian Universalist Association's Women and Religion Committee.

Under Northern Skies met every full and new moon to honor earth-based spirituality with an emphasis on the feminine and was open to new members every fall. After a commitment ritual in late fall, the group closed to new members for the remainder of the year.

The circle operated under shared leadership, with members taking turns leading the ritual. While the basic format remained constant from circle to circle, the specifics of the circle were up to each woman or group of women who led. Occasionally there was no designated leader or planned ritual. Such times were referred to as pot-luck circles—the ritual being dependent on what each participant brought that particular evening. For

Sharon Bishop attended a workshop on rituals, I think at General Assembly in 1982. She decided she wanted to help create new and meaningful rituals at First Universalist. I was in seminary at the time. She asked if we could design one.

The first Solstice Circle was held on Dec. 21, 1982. There were about 16 of us. We had one large candle in the center of the circle. We opened with "Raise the Fruit" by Meridel Le Sueur. We danced and sang to "We Are Dancing Sarah's Circle." We shared stories of Light and Dark from our lives and closed with a poem by T.S. Elliot.

After Susan Milnor came, she added the choral voices and the movement choir. In the late 1990s we added the intergenerational dimension, including the acting out of a folktale about the light and the dark and the light sticks.

—the Reverend Laurie Bushbaum

many women, deeply moving experiences and insights took place within the safety of the circle.

Winter Solstice

Solstice celebrations began in 1982 when a group of women from the ritual circle identified a desire to celebrate this winter holiday. From its beginnings with a small group of women and the guidance of the Reverend Laurie Bushbaum, then a ministerial student, the celebration grew to be one of the most-attended services offered at First Universalist. The sanctuary filled to capacity with congregants and members of the larger community all gathered to honor the darkness and celebrate the return of the light.

The solstice service itself varies from year to year, with stories, music or short homilies related to a chosen theme, but certain elements of the ritual remain constant. The solstice celebrations begin with a labyrinth walk in the Social Hall or in silence with seated meditation in preparation for the larger solstice service. Another prelude to the solstice service is the ritual meal of cold finger food brought by participants. An empty bowl placed on the serving table reminds all that what one has is sufficient.

Congregants are then welcomed into the sanctuary by women dressed in white, who bless each person with saltwater and evergreen branches. The ritual begins by calling the directions and casting the circle, invoking the spirits of the East, South, West, North and Center. The ritual then progresses from light to darkness, then back to light again. The spreading of the light, with the entire sanctuary in candlelight, is one of the most moving moments of the evening. The celebration culminates in the triumphant return of the sun, with chanting and dancing that continues in the Social Hall, with music, more dancing, and ginger cookies.

The Labyrinth Circle

On June 21, 1998, a 36-foot canvas labyrinth was dedicated at First Universalist Church. This canvas labyrinth, a replica of the labyrinth design at Chartres Cathedral, was lent to the church by the Reverend

Barbara Kellett, a community minister affiliated with First Universalist. In 1999, a small group began hosting open labyrinth walks that were attended by people from the congregation as well as people from the wider community. The labyrinth was also made available for New Year's Eve open walks and Coming of Age presentations. For several years, the Labyrinth Circle made presentations at Prairie Star District Conferences and in 2000, a labyrinth walk was first added to the Winter Solstice celebration.

By 2002, the labyrinth practice at First Universalist was engrained in the spiritual practices of the church. Labyrinth walks were used in Religious Education classes, Coming of Age ceremonies, the Unity Summer program, on New Year's Eve, and at the AUW Women's Retreat. Setting up the large canvas labyrinth took time and effort to prepare for each event and a permanent labyrinth, to be etched into the terrazzo floor in the Social Hall, was proposed. Fundraising and generous donations made the permanent installation possible. On March 26, 2005, the etched labyrinth on the Social Hall floor was dedicated.

Cycle of Life
During the ministry of the Reverends Frank Rivas and Kate Tucker, joys and sorrows of congregants were shared from the pulpit and the congregation greeted people sitting near them. Each worship service ended with the congregation joining hands and singing "Go Now in Peace." Many of these communal practices might have surprised the more formal congregants of 100 years earlier, but the new traditions were emblematic of the focus on community and relationship that increasingly characterized First Universalist Church.

—Pamela Vincent and Kathy Coskran

Installations and Ordinations

Rituals are intentional acts, often symbolic, usually repeated, that enact or try to invoke some larger reality or truth. . . . Take the Thanksgiving ritual of feasting. On one level, it seeks to tie us to the story of the Pilgrims, to the history of a people. On another level, it urges us into a spiritual stance, inviting us to become creatures grateful for the giftedness of life and the bounty of the earth. A third level, though, captures the deepest meaning. In these Thanksgiving rituals, we seek to experience the spirit of agreement and, yes, of compromise that allows us to live together in families and communities and societies. Rituals are acts which, when they work, help us cross a threshold from one internal space to another. With religious rituals . . . that crossing is usually from the mundane to the sacred.
—the Reverend Susan Milnor, 1991

The Rite of Ordination of ministers is a sacred responsibility, reserved solely for the congregation in Unitarian Universalism. These pictures show the ordination of two members of First Universalist: the Reverend Gretchen Thompson (above in front of podium) and the Reverend Harlan Limpert (right being congratulated by Mildred Olson and Marion Griffith).

Installations occur after a minister is called to service in a new congregation. It signifies the symbiotic nature of the relationship and begins the mutual covenant of responsibility between the two bodies—minister and members of the congregation.

FAITH DEVELOPMENT
RELIGIOUS AWARENESS, NOT INDOCTRINATION

It is important for us to realize that our program of religious education should not be designed primarily to produce Universalists and Unitarians in our own image or in the image of a preceding generation. It should be designed to produce young people who shall be so equipped as to be capable of becoming religious liberals in their own right and in their own age. That is, the aim of our religious education should be not to transmit a theology to children but to help them in living their own lives and in preparing for an adulthood which shall include vital ethical and religious awareness, rather than an inheritance only.
—the Reverend Carl Olson, 1955

Classroom circa 1955

In the early days the Bible was used liberally in the church. Sunday school students were expected to memorize and recite Bible verses, the Lord's Prayer, Psalms, and the Ten Commandments. This emphasis on the Bible was consistent with Universalist theology at the time. As times changed, however, so did religious education.

The Council of Liberal Churches was born in 1953 and produced materials—begun earlier under the watch of Sophia Fahs in the Unitarian faith—that encouraged creativity and questioning. First Universalist purchased dramatic plays such as *The Trial of Michael Servetus* and *Socrates*, which came with leader guides to aid students in discussing the great existential questions.

Throughout the 1950s the church gave students Bibles donated by the AUW on Children's Day. Early in his ministry, the Reverend John Cummins persuaded the AUW to buy copies of *The World Bible* by Robert O. Ballou instead of traditional Bibles. Ballou's Bible offered students a way to study the great religions of the world in addition to Christianity and was a precursor to "The Church Across the Street" curriculum in which students visited other churches every Sunday. By 2009 the study of the diversity of religious beliefs was part of the seventh-grade curriculum, "Neighboring Faiths."

In November 1971, the About Your Sexuality (AYS) program was started in selected Unitarian Universalist churches around the country. It was rare then to talk openly about heterosexual sex, and it was radical to discuss the sexual practices of homosexual partners. The curriculum was based on the

Children in Protestant families were expected to attend Sunday school. My only recollections of that church are learning to sing "Jesus Loves Me" and being expelled from summer Bible school because I cut up the crayons. Sometime in the early '40s, my parents had heard Dr. Olson conduct the funeral service for a friend of my parents. My parents were impressed with the sensitivity and understanding with which Dr. Olson delivered the eulogy. I joined the church in 1953.
—Verna Rausch, quoted in a 1992 booklet of recollections from 20-year

A 7th-grade classroom taught by Miss Marabeth Hobbs, circa 1955

In the early '50s I taught a class of teenagers—my son was one—a course from a book by Sophia Fahs, "The Church Across the Street," from which I learned a great deal. Since it was a small group we could travel by station wagon to those churches: Greek Orthodox, Roman Catholic, Lutheran, etc., to Mormon, Christian Science, The Great I Am. Some of the time parents joined us. We would discuss these religions between visits. This went on for two years. It was one of the most enlightening experiences in bringing up four children. All four are liberals.

—Beverly Sommers, 1992 booklet

notion that sexual behavior should not be isolated and should be consistent with one's value system.

First Universalist was chosen for an AYS pilot program and, as a result, religious education director Nancy Carlson became a mentor to teachers in Minnesota and surrounding states. As she explained at the time, "This course is not on the nuts and bolts of sex, but on human sexual behavior. It deals with concepts and attitudes and people as human beings."

The curriculum evolved to "Our Whole Lives (OWL)," a year-long class for eighth graders with a focus on helping participants gain the knowledge, values and skills that lead to healthy, responsible lives.

In 2006 the congregation engaged in an extensive discernment process that focused on religious education as a whole and, as a result, changed the name of the Religious Education Program to Lifespan Faith Development. By 2009 Lifespan Faith Development had become increasingly diverse in providing opportunities for education, spiritual growth and community service. The four- and five-year-olds focused on the diversity of family compositions and experiences and the congregation's commitment to welcoming all families through the "Families All Matter Anti-Bias Book Project." Elementary children also gather monthly for Children's Chapel.

In the Coming of Age Program, ninth graders are asked to consider God, death, morality, ethics and more in a quest to write a spiritual statement about what they believe. Their faith statements, presented to the community in the spring, represent where they are on their spiritual journey, not their final destination. They receive a rose at this ceremony, just as they did at their child dedication, but with the thorns intact because they now know how to protect themselves.

The Youth Cultural Exchange provides a unique opportunity for First Universalist young people to connect with people their age in significantly different life situations. In addition, many youth—inside and outside the congregation—have participated in Unity Summer Leadership, a life-changing experience.

The arc of religious education programming for children and young people over 150 years is another window into the evolution of theology and practice at First Universalist Church and the response of a liberal religion to the times we live in.

—*Mary Junge*

Beverly Barker leads a nursery classroom

Rainbow Path
The Reverend Laurie Bushbaum developed two years of curriculum on the Rainbow Path as Contract Minister for Children and Youth. Each of the seven UU Principles is linked to a color of the rainbow.

Red: Respect all beings
Orange: Offer fair and kind treatment to all
Yellow: Yearn to learn
Green: Grow in spirit and mind
Blue: Believe in our ideas and act on them
Indigo: Insist on peace, freedom and justice
Violet: Value the connections in creation

1885 Sunday School

A 1885 Sunday school class at Church of the Redeemer, taught by W. P. Roberts (left), with Mrs. Evelyn Burt (right) as singing director, consisted of 19 high-school-aged girls, including Effie Ames, daughter of a Minneapolis mayor (middle).

It was November 1951 when my husband and I joined. One time, a parents' meeting was announced for the purpose of organizing a Religious Education Committee to plan the curriculum and activities. Only two parents showed: Elise Hoppe and myself. She became chairperson and I assumed the role of religious education director.

One Christmas I asked Emile Hastings and his wife, Lillian, both artists who volunteered in the Church School, if a large window could be built for the front of the church for a Christmas program. Emile built a beautiful huge window frame and the students presented a series of scenes and sketches entitled "The Windows of the Earth," about children and religions around the world.

—Viola K. Dreessen, 1992 booklet

The Barker family, at Lee's ordination

Religious Educators

After Lionel and Beverly Barker became the parents of Gail, Lee and Hope, they were looking for a church to reflect their personal philosophy. An article in *Time* magazine referred to "those hard working Universalists," so they requested literature. "After reading the pamphlets," Beverly recalled in 1992, "we knew this was the right church for us and joined in 1953." Beverly became active in the church school, eventually becoming the Religious Education (RE) director, from 1959 to 1964. All of their children became active Unitarian Universalists. Son Lee, a UU minister, was ordained at First Universalist and served as president of the Meadville Lombard Theological School.

Religious Education directors following Beverly Barker include:
- Luella Neustrom, organized evening church school to alleviate crowding on Sundays and created a weekly newsletter for RE teachers;
- Nancy Carlson, director for 18 years, remembered for starting the Christmas tradition of Joyballs and the Maypole dance;
- Meg Riley, started an RE advisory committee as well as a long-term committee to assess curriculum elements;
- Ginger Luke, known for storytelling and ritualizing worship;
- Bilinda Straight, brought world views to children;
- the Reverend Laurie Bushbaum, introduced the Rainbow Path, with a focus on the seven UU principles, and the Christmas pageant;
- Shari Goff, bolstered the church with community-building;
- Heidi Mastrud, responsible for overall leadership of education programming for children, youth and adults as the first director of congregational life;
- Katie Heaton, youth and young adult ministries coordinator.

MUSIC
A SONG IS RISING

Spirit of Life, come unto me; sing in my heart all the stirrings of compassion.' When we sing this song together, we experience a unity that's beyond words. When we sing together, the music we make transcends time, language, age, race, gender, and all other categories that might divide us. When we sing together, we create a symphony of wholeness that exceeds the sum of our solo parts.
—the Reverend Kate Tucker,
in her 2005 sermon "A Song is Rising"

Music has always had a prominent and beloved role in the life of First Universalist Church. When the first church building was completed in 1866, it included the first complete church organ in Minneapolis. When the congregation outgrew that building, they built an impressive stone church with seating for 1,000 and an organ to match. Charles Marsh, who served as church organist for 11 years, played the instrument at the dedication of the building on July 10, 1876.

Fire badly damaged the church in January 1888, but rebuilding and enlarging came swiftly. When the rebuilt church was dedicated in 1889, it included an $11,000 organ.

Perhaps the best known organist was Emil Oberhoffer, who was also the first conductor of the Minneapolis Symphony Orchestra when it was founded in 1903. Music was a high priority for the church at that time. During 1907-08, Oberhoffer's last year, payments to the organist and choir of four paid singers amounted to almost a quarter of the total revenue.

After years with majestic pipe organs, by 1958 the choir of a dozen or so dedicated musicians sang around a Hammond organ at the front of the church directed by organist Grace Ernst during her 11-year tenure.

An account of the music program by Barbara Whipple, who joined the choir in 1953, from the AUW history *100 Years of Liberation*, tells of choir director Curt Anderson's decision to move the choir and organ to the balcony of the church at 5000 Girard without first getting the permission

We gratefully acknowledged the generous gift of the pipe organ, the first to be brought to Minneapolis. It is difficult to express in fitting terms the notable influence its possession . . . has had on the attractiveness of our services. We have been especially fortunate in having such directors as Leeds, Marsh, Harmsen, Chick, Woodruff, Oberhoffer and Jones, and choirs of exceptional proficiency.
—Major William D. Hale,
50th anniversary remarks

The donor of organ and bells [William D. Washburn] has recently added to our debt to him by selecting and uniting Tennyson's grand poem for the New Year, "Ring Out Wild Bells," to the majestic Cujus Amimam of Rossini's "Stabat Mater," making together one of the most inspiring chorals . . . to be heard in any of the greatest churches . . . We should rename it "The Choral of the Church of the Redeemer" and provide that it be sung at least once every holiday season as long as our organization exists.
—Major William D. Hale, 50th anniversary remarks

of the Board of Trustees. "This caused quite a stir," Whipple wrote. "The church was growing and Curt was a good director, so the choir grew also. He liked to improvise on the organ when there was an appropriate place in the order of service. His improvisation would meander around and eventually resolve to an ending. But there were a few times when he couldn't think how to end it, and it would go on longer than necessary. The choir, which was hidden from view in the balcony, could smile and enjoy Curt's difficulty without giving away that he was really playing a Bach prelude."

Jim Bonn, who followed Curt as music director, convinced the church to buy the Yamaha piano that is still in use. Subsequent director Jim Hart introduced the choir to a lively new type of music, including Scott Joplin's "Treemonisha."

The next director was Jim Reilly who, according to long-time chorist Janet Chandler, preferred more esoteric and subdued music. "He wanted to support new composers, and convinced the music committee to commission two compositions for the choir. My recollection is that they were quite difficult to sing. One of the composers was Libby Larsen, who has since become prominent on the local music scene." Reilly also introduced the Women's Composer series.

David Livingston, who followed Reilly, had a particular gift for integrating Sunday morning music with the worship service. He was instrumental in starting the Universal Jazz group. Livingston was proficient on the alto sax and recorder and often played one or the other while the congregation sang.

In 1993 the UUA produced a new hymnal, *Singing the Living Tradition*, that included "A Core of Silence," with words and music by Reilly. Church members and friends purchased 400 hymnals for the church by donating $25 per book to honor special people in their lives. Member Carol Jackson did calligraphy for the bookplates. A publication celebration and concert was held at the Fitzgerald Theater in St. Paul.

In 1992 John Jensen came to First Universalist as pianist and became music director in 1996, the same year that Janice Hunton became choral director. Jensen became well-known in the region as a solo performer, ensemble player, accompanist and recording artist, equally at home with classical repertoire and jazz.

Hunton was a member of the Dale Warland Singers and on the faculty of the music department at the Perpich Center for Arts Education. Jensen and Hunton, together with children's choir director Mary Bohman, built a music program that included adult and children's choirs, the Universal Jazz Band, the Universal Folk Band and the Universal Rock Band.

—*Marie Nordberg*

Long-time member Janet Chandler, who sang in the choir from the 1960s until 1993, fondly remembers pianist Eileen Reagan (top). "She had a beautiful and elegant touch that we all admired," said Chandler.

Children's choir director Mary Bohman

Music director John Jensen, on piano

The Arts:
Beauty Before Us

*Beauty is before me, and
Beauty behind me,
above me and below me
hovers the beautiful.
I am surrounded by it,
I am immersed in it.
In my youth, I am
aware of it,
and, in old age,
I shall walk quietly the
beautiful trail.
In beauty it is begun.
In beauty, it is ended.*

—from the Navajo Indians of North America, from *Singing the Living Tradition,* number 682

Chalice created by Christina Blum

Early church photographs show that aesthetic considerations were integral to worship at the First Universalist Society and the Church of the Redeemer. The Reverend James Tuttle spoke of the beauty of the flowers prepared by the women of the church. A 1910 annual Flower Mission report indicated the group had provided flowers every Sunday, with special displays for Easter, Memorial Day, Harvest Sunday, and Christmas. Repeated reference was made to the grand pipe organ made of black walnut. In addition memorials honoring women often were gifts to the church in the form of fine china or exquisite silver tea services. The Reverend Marion Shutter refers to the Needlework Guild's annual exhibit, evidence that art displays were part of early church life.

The role of creating beauty within the church was formalized in the mid-1960s by the creation of the Visual Arts Committee, giving members an opportunity to offer their aesthetic gifts and energy to enhancing each church building and to creating lovely worship space.

The 1993 move to a larger sanctuary at 3400 Dupont Avenue South presented several artistic opportunities. Flower arrangements needed to be larger, a chalice harmonious to the space needed to be created, and the chancel needed to be created in a way that reflected the Universalist faith and that provided an aesthetic backdrop for the art and decoration.

Flowers
The flower arrangements prepared by a member of the Visual Arts Committee each Sunday create an atmosphere of peace and calm, or beauty and joy, in the sanctuary. The arrangements also offer congregants an opportunity to honor an occasion or an individual by funding the flowers for a Sunday service.

Liturgical Pieces
In the late 1980s, the Visual Arts Committee commissioned Steve Arnold to build a lectern and two matching pedestals to replace a cumbersome speaker's stand. The delicate design of the lectern was enhanced with a collection of textiles developed by Lael Eginton and Ruth Arnold that add grace and beauty to the worship space.

This We Believe

In the 1990s, church member and sculptor Christina Blum created a chalice to stand on its own on the chancel. Blum studied the building design and incorporated the curved rungs from the stairwell banister for the stand, used a variety of metals to form the chalice, and provided a glass piece containing oil for the flame.

The Cummins Room
The Reverend John and Dru Cummins, always advocates for the arts, funded renovation of the chapel at 3400 Dupont Avenue South so the church would have an attractive room for small services and special events. They wanted something beautiful to represent Unitarian Universalism (UU) within the space and, with the help of the Visual Arts committee, commissioned Heidi Hoy, an artist with UU roots, to create a metal sculpture using a UU symbol that had been developed earlier by church member Emile Hastings, modified by Cummins. The chapel was named for the Cummins and dedicated in their honor.

The Space, Planning, Improvement, Facilities, and Furnishings Committee (SPIFF), an offshoot of the Visual Arts and Building and Grounds Committees, completed the chapel renovation with fresh paint, a new carpet, photos of First Universalist ministers, a photo of both Cummins, and other historical information. SPIFF held a second ceremony in 2003 to honor the Cummins and the improvements that had been made. In 2006, paintings of Unity House and the Girard Church were framed and added to the Cummins Room.

Permanent Art Installations
Artist David Baldwin was commissioned by capital campaign co-chairs Harlan Limpert and Bette DeMars in 2001 to create a large calligraphy piece to include the name of each individual who had contributed to the campaign. Other permanent art pieces include a sculpture created and donated by church member Earl Masterson and three Hmong textiles that were included in Khang Vang's 1990 exhibit.

Exterior Space
Believing that being a good neighbor and a welcoming presence to the broader community are integral to the church's mission, church volunteers have given their time and energy to beautify the exterior of church buildings. Karen Olson sewed colorful UU banners that were displayed on poles at the Girard Church. The tradition of welcoming

UU artist Heidi Hoy, pictured with the Reverend John Cummins, created several permanent pieces for church spaces.

Hoy created a chalice for the Cummins Room, commissioned by Anne and Hal Ransom, to rest on a wooden base built by Doug Hicks. For the Sesquicentennial, Hoy was commissioned to develop a large UU sculpture to hang over the chancel.

Following the sudden death of board member Gracie Carpenter, artist and friend Jane Evershed (pictured above left with Carpenter's children), painted a colorful piece that reflected Carpenter's generous spirit and charismatic personality and represented her life-long advocacy for children.

banners continued with a variety of colors and designs that highlighted the Dupont church. Christine Bailey developed a garden plan for the north side of the church, Peter Crane developed the Peace Garden, and Douglas Owens-Pike developed the Chalice Room Garden.

Art Exhibits

Throughout the years, art exhibits have given congregants and visitors a chance to view a variety of art forms and to support artists. In 1988, member Fran Addington organized a cross-cultural exhibit, attended by artists and school children. Ten years later the Reverend Laurie Bushbaum developed a major textile exhibit, "Whispering Threads," which featured textiles and board paintings created by women from Zimbabwe. Congregants enthusiastically supported the Zimbabwe Artist Project, with exhibit proceeds topping all previous sales. The Visual Arts Committee purchased two textiles to hang in the library to honor Sharon and Dan Bishop for all they had done to develop the library. To coordinate with activities surrounding the sesquicentennial's Darwin events in 2009, artist Lynn Felman presented her work "Portraits Inspired by Population Genetics."

Art exhibits also offered church members an opportunity to display their art work, many for the first time. Many photographers in the congregation have shared their talents. As part of the AUW's centennial celebration, Bette DeMars worked with the AUW to develop "Art for Art." Women artists from church donated a piece of their art and weekly bidding took place. Profits from the show went toward several beautiful pieces for the church—two glass creations for water, a lectern cloth, minister stoles, and a banner.

Holiday Decorations

The winter holiday decorations created by the Visual Arts Committee reflect the diverse sources the church draws on for wisdom and a sense of the holy. The sanctuary has been transformed into a simple forest scene, has been festooned with solar shields, with fruit wreaths and topiaries, has represented Christmas scenes from around the world, and has featured pastel peace cranes floating from hoops. The emphasis is on creating simple tableaux that invite the eye and nourish the spirit.

—Bette DeMars

Congregational Polity

Subscriptions made in the office of board president Dorilus Morrison on one evening in 1875 for the completion of the Church of the Redeemer. This was a glimpse of the way members gave freely as an indication of their beliefs.

As the Reverend John Cummins liked to remind First Universalist congregants, if you want to know what you believe in, "all you need to do is look at your check stubs. What you spend your time and money on, that is what you believe in." Many of the earliest trustees invested both time and money in their Universalist beliefs.

The early trustees were largely men (only a handful of women appeared on the board until the 1970s), who were active in business, civic affairs and politics. For example, George Chowen, the Hennepin County Register of Deeds, signed the articles of incorporation for First Universalist in 1864, and served as the church clerk for many years. Prominent lawyer F.R.E. Cornell, a member of the first Board of Trustees, was a member of the state legislature, served as state attorney general, and was eventually an associate justice of the Minnesota Supreme Court. He was named one of the 100 most influential attorneys in state history, according to *Minnesota Law & Politics*, and was

The first Board of Trustees consisted of William Garland, F.R.E. Cornell, Thomas Perkins, William D. Washburn, and H.J. Plumer. Officers also included Secretary William Cornell and Treasurer George Crocker, "all of whom shall be elected annually by ballot at the regular annual meeting," which was to be the first Monday of October. Any person was eligible to become a member of the Society after written application to the trustees and a vote of a majority of the members at any regular meeting. The next session was called for the first Monday in November, to be held at Cataract House at 7 p.m.

an active abolitionist who successfully argued for the freedom of a slave woman who had been brought north. In a time before air transportation, the automobile, the telephone, computers, even typewriters, it is hard to imagine how these men found time to be hands-on trustees.

Over time, many of the early trustees built substantial business empires and personal fortunes. Not only did they make gifts and bequests to the church, their pew rental payments for prominent seats provided good income to the church. They set a powerful example for the trustees who followed and created a culture of strong, responsible lay leadership.

Expenses and Revenue: 1928

The financial statements published in church yearbooks revealed a consistent concern about money, a perennial concern for trustees everywhere. In times when the national economy went through regular boom and bust cycles, early trustees were concerned with building a large endowment for the church and with investing it as safely as possible.

In 1928, as an example, subscriptions exceeded pew rentals as income. In detailed information about collections, just over two-thirds came from a morning service and almost one-third came from an evening service. A loan was borrowed from endowment and bequest funds. Interest was earned from investing endowment and bequest funds, less than a year before the stock market crash.

On the expense side of things, the church had purchased a motion picture projector and was paying for films, an operator and the upkeep of the projector. These expenses appear on the annual reports for a number of years. The 1928 budget would equal $801,090 in 2008 dollars.

Expenses and Revenue: 1962

The Reverend John Cummins had just been called as minister. Both the income and expenses for that year reflect proceeds from the sale of a parsonage owned by the church. Subscriptions were now called pledges. The 1962 budget would be $905,622 in 2008 dollars, but was inflated by the parsonage transaction.

We the subscribers feeling desirous "to grow in grace, and in the knowledge of our Lord and Saviour Jesus Christ" do hereby form ourselves into a Society, that we may be helps to each other, and that by our united energies we may better serve the purposes of religion and truth. We cheerfully and sincerely adopt and subscribe as the basis of our government the following . . .
—The Preamble to the Constitution of the First Universalist Society, adopted unanimously, February 6, 1864.

Organizational Structure

The management structure of the church evolved over 150 years, but much remained constant as well. In 2009 trustees still had fiduciary responsibility for the church and oversaw the business affairs of the church, but with some actions specifically reserved for members, such as electing trustees, calling and dismissing ministers, and adopting or amending bylaws.

The annual meeting in 1964 saw a change in trustees' relationship to program committees. In addition to being responsible for church financial controls, the board members now needed to stay informed about the actions and needs of their respective committee assignments —a substantial additional time commitment.

By 1981 it was obvious that the governance model giving the board enormous control over the program areas of the church was not working. The Program Council, chaired by the vice-president of the board and comprised of the chairs of the committees, was created. In a report to the board, ministerial intern Peter J. Luton wrote: "The council will free up the Trustees from direct responsibility for programming and allow them to concentrate upon policies, procedures, administration, budgeting, goal setting and the general health of the institution."

However, an examination of board goals throughout the 1980s and 1990s shows the trustees still quite embedded in church programs and operations, despite the evolution of the Program Council to the All Church Council. By 2000 it was clear that the distinctive roles of trustees and All Church Council members were poorly defined and the Unitarian Universalist Association was recommending that large UU congregations consider moving to policy governance. Policy governance offered the advantage of clearly defined roles for the staff of the church and for the board, and it promised to free the board from managing the day-to-day operations of the church. The board could concentrate on monitoring the financial condition of the church, communicating with the congregation, setting short and long range goals, and monitoring the effectiveness of the senior minister and the staff in achieving the congregational vision. A governance task force was formed in 2002 to examine the current structure and bring recommendations to the board and to the congregation.

By 1919, pew rentals were by far the largest source of funding, with collections being a distant second. There was a bit of income from invested endowments, but a crash a few years earlier had greatly diminished those. On the expense side of things, staff was the biggest slice of the pie. It is interesting to note that the proportions held steady for over 100 years.

In 1905, the budget—converted to 2008 U.S. dollars—equaled $774,301.

For the 2008-2009 year, the budget was $1,234,827. Expenses were largely for expanded programming in religious education and increased staff support. A significant source of income was rental from a charter school.

We did the challenging, unglamorous work of changing the way the church operates and governs itself. After having studied and flirted with it for many years, we adopted a paradigm called "policy governance" wherein the Board of Trustees retains its fiduciary responsibility and policy-making authority but delegates operating authority and responsibility to the senior minister. . . . This represents a dramatic change from the way we'd governed ourselves previously.
—President Sue Schiess' Report to the Annual Meeting, 2009

The movement toward policy governance was not an easy one. There was anxiety that policy governance might not fit the grassroots sense of empowerment in the congregation. With the delegation of the day-to-day management of the church through the senior minister to the staff, the board had to develop a level of trust and discipline not to deal with tactical issues that were delegated to staff. The board needed to turn its attention to setting strategic direction, monitoring the effectiveness of the senior minister and staff and communicating more effectively with congregants.

In 2007 the trustees voted to move toward policy governance and appointed another task force to draft bylaw changes and a Governing Policy Handbook. In Fall 2008, the board as a whole reviewed the proposed bylaw changes and recommended their adoption to the congregation. In January 2009, the bylaw changes were adopted at a special congregational meeting, making the transition complete.
—Judy Goebel

The increasingly co-ed face of the Board of Trustees was a significant change from the 1940s (above) to the 1970s (left).

This We Believe
Words from the pulpit

Reading the sermons preached at First Universalist over 150 years is both fascinating and revealing. All the ministers were eloquent, well-educated, and grounded in Universalist history—and they were also men and women of their times. The earliest ministers, the Reverends James Tuttle and Marion Shutter, referred to the Bible frequently, spoke of the afterlife, and assumed a liberal Christian base for their theology. Tuttle's debate about evolution with the Reverend Herman Bisbee, the minister across the river, is something of an embarrassment to Unitarian Universalists in 2009. It is clear now that Tuttle was on the wrong side of that question, but his position *was* in line with then-current Universalist leanings.

The Reverend Carl Olson continued to refer to Scripture readings in his sermons, but his essential vision was of an inclusive religion of love and hope, a message that would resonate and be articulated for the next 75 years. The Reverend John Cummins broadened his text to include prophets from any age or religion and added a level of social activism to his message. The Reverends Susan Milnor and Terry Sweetser used story, both metaphorical and personal, to amplify the many aspects of their message of love and hope. The Reverend Frank Rivas referred to the Catholicism of his childhood and his study of Eastern religions to expand the ways one might seek spiritual connection. The Reverend Kate Tucker's ability to recognize connections and to reveal grace and depth in small moments was a touchstone of her message of peace and redemption, love and hope.

These are broad, general statements. Each minister was so much more than can be represented in a single sentence or in the few, out-of-context sermon excerpts that follow. But the flavor is there and the passion and the commitment to the search for truth and meaning in the times they—and we—lived in.

The Reverend Terry Sweetser in the pulpit at 5000 Girard Avenue

We Unitarian Universalists like to know the truth, but we have a little more trouble believing in our power. We need to remind ourselves, time and time again that when people come together with open minds and hearts they bring along a lot of power. When those minds and hearts converge, the power to solve problems is tremendous.
—the Reverend Terry Sweetser, "Stepping Out of the Lie: The 1992 Presidential Election"

The Reverend James Tuttle In the Pulpit

Copies of the sermons of First Universalist's first settled minister, the Reverend Joseph W. Keyes, have not survived, but much can be learned from the Reverend James Tuttle's sermons and writings. He was a beloved and well-respected minister throughout the community, whose poetic love of nature often found its way into his writing.

Tuttle wrote *The Field and the Fruit: A Memorial of 25 Years of Ministry with the Church of the Redeemer.* Within those pages is a long foreword telling of the early church and 12 sermons, which represent his years there. "I have more and more, as time has passed, felt the necessity of taking the chief emphasis from doctrine, and placing it upon conduct."

In spite of his disdain for some of the science of his day, he once remarked that he did not fear science and skepticism, for he believed that it was part of the nature of humanity to be spiritual. Once he mentioned pagans in a sermon, saying that all humanity has within it the light, and that if that light shines forth then salvation is available to all.

Tuttle had a genuine love of nature and compared its capacity to regenerate itself to that of the spiritual world. In a sermon called "Beauty to Ashes," in a dedication of the church after the fire of 1888, he suggested that all in the moral and spiritual world can be called ashes, but that it will be transformed to beauty at the end. In that same sermon he said:

> *There is no death! The dust we tread*
> *Shall change beneath the summer showers*
> *To Golden grain and mellow fruit,*
> *Or rainbow tinted flowers.*

He wrestled with the relationship of sin and punishment in his sermons. Tuttle felt that all souls were made ready for salvation and that repentance was inevitable. At one point he said those who refused to repent would simply be destroyed, then on another occasion said that even they would be brought to salvation.

—*Jessica Wicks*

About Salvation

And now is the final question: Does God's promise to give 'beauty for ashes' end with this life? Does the all-pervading, all-conquering, and all-regenerating law we have traced through Nature up to Nature's God stop at the grave? The church we have built here, our service of Dedication, our hopes and prayers, our love, our faith, this Bible open before me, and the voices of the earth answer, 'No.'

The Mission

Christianity sends us out of ourselves, out of our homes, out of our churches, out of our [political] parties, out of our nationalities even, on missions of reform; it sends us out of everywhere into everywhere where good is to be done, where the ignorant are to be taught, the hungry fed, the naked clothed, the sorrowful comforted, and transgressors converted. The New Testament does not spend its breath so much on the saved as on the unsaved, not so much to make feasts for the rich as for the poor. It does not teach us to sing hallelujahs over saints in their rocking-chairs so much as over the victories which sinners win through repentance.

. . .

What is wealth? It is a fold, but not for those alone who have wealth. It is not to gratify its possessors merely. It is an outreaching and down-reaching helpfulness to persons less favored. No man is rich who does not share his treasures and his comforts with the poor. What is society? It is a fold, and yet not a fold for protecting the best people only. It exists, or should exist, for all who need its advantages, all who can be brought into it from the unorganized masses.

. . .

Any helpful power, any excellence, any superiority of gift which any person or body of persons possesses, lays on such person or body a corresponding obligation to extend it, to distribute it as far as possible. The young man who, more blessed in this respect than other young men around him, has been to college and has returned with his diploma, is but poorly educated and shows but little gratitude for his superior opportunities, if he does not humbly strive to make himself henceforth a light in the dark places of society.

Eternity must be time extended. We shall probably keep up our connection with the world through our memory, if in no other way. And our character shall, for a time, at least, bear something of the form and substance we carried with us from the earth.
—the Reverend James Tuttle

The Evolution Debate

After Charles Darwin's *On the Origin of Species* was published in 1859—the same year First Universalist was founded—it did not take long for the theory to trickle across the Atlantic, since it was an overnight best-seller. It captured the attention of naturalist Ralph Waldo Emerson. His interest, in turn, inspired a fellow New Englander, the Reverend Herman Bisbee, who brought the ideas with him to the pioneering Universalist settlement in St. Anthony, across the river from the First Universalist Society of Minneapolis.

The subsequent heresy trial of Bisbee is considered a black mark on Universalism, embroiling as a major player the Reverend James Tuttle. It is a well-known story in national Universalist lore, told well in the Prairie Star District documentary *Heritage of Heresy: Bisbee & Tuttle*.

> *"The theological agitations we all have passed through have of course shaken from me many ideas and doctrines I once entertained."*
> —the Reverend James Tuttle

Bisbee was not necessarily an agitator, but he did not shirk from stirring up publicity. He was brash and intelligent enough to stand up to authority if he felt it was warranted. At the time, in the 1860s, Universalists were firmly grounded in Christian beliefs. While wanting to avoid forced creeds, and promoting the still controversial idea of a loving God and universal salvation, Universalists were interested in maintaining a reverence for the Bible as a primary source of wisdom. Bisbee—who also was prescient in his strong interest in giving women the right to vote—believed that Darwin's theory of evolution was a worthy topic of discussion in the pulpit. Where he seemed to cross a line was in stepping across the river to publicly discuss why he believed strict Christian adherence to the Bible's version of creation, as Tuttle clearly espoused, was inadequate.

Tuttle, an older man of strong principle, took offense and volleyed back. This became great entertainment for 1872 Minneapolis, where the Pence Opera House was filled to capacity to hear the debates, which escalated in the newspapers.

Eventually Universalist leaders felt the need to step in. Bisbee was censured after three of his local Minnesota peers—all men who had clashed with Bisbee previously—proclaimed him guilty of heresy. Bisbee's faithful congregation remained with him for several years as members of an independent church entity, until the disenfranchised minister left to attend Harvard Divinity School. Bisbee did not live long enough to see his views validated over time. His loyal St. Anthony congregants could not find a replacement after he left, but nonetheless most of them refused to join the congregation across the river.

Tuttle is the curious one in the controversy. Although he stood up against what he considered an affront to his turf and his beliefs after Bisbee struck, he also was the one who recruited his successor, the Reverend Marion Shutter, to the Church of the Redeemer. That turned out to be ironic. Shutter did as much as any other Universalist to popularize the notion that Darwin was right. He too strongly advocated —with more success than Bisbee—that evolution did not defy belief in God, the Bible, or the fundamental conviction that everyone had the right to come to their own beliefs in their own way and in their own time. In fact, it was said to be Shutter's crisis of faith after the death of his wife, along with his own reading of Darwin, that led him to abandon his Baptist faith. And it was Tuttle who convinced Shutter to join Universalism.

—*Mikki Morrissette*

The Reverend Herman Bisbee

Tuttle vs. Bisbee: a sample

Tuttle, as reported in the Minneapolis Tribune, *January 16, 1872*
Shall we be called superstitious if we hold to our belief that the germs of life were found in God? There is something in man besides chemical properties. Life the chemist cannot give. How do these materials come together so as to produce life? A watch we know is made of metals, but it required the watchmaker to construct it and give it proper conditions. So it required a God to form the human body, and when formed, a God must give it life. . . . If for every leaf of science we must tear a leaf from the Bible, our path of knowledge will be dark indeed.

Bisbee, as reported January 23, 1872
I have been a believer in the infallibility of the Bible and hence I can easily comprehend those who feel regret and even horror when a passage of the Bible is doubted. . . . I do not think the writer of Genesis designed to impose upon men. He wrote the best he knew. Our best is to do better. Shall we then throw the Bible away? No. Is the golden rule less golden? The beatitudes less beautiful? The 23rd Psalm less comforting? The life of Jesus less sweet and tender? Flowers less fragrant because they are born in a world not all flowers? Says Mr. Tuttle, "If for every leaf of science we must tear a leaf from the Bible our path will be dark indeed." The Bible contains some leaves not so valuable as others.

Upon going to Pence Opera House one Sunday afternoon I found it crowded with members of the St. Anthony Church and the Church of the Redeemer. An aunt who had accompanied me said: "Cordelia, how dare you bring me to such a sink of iniquity [sic]—just dealings with the devil, that's all!

—from "Reminiscences" by Mrs. M.S. Staring

THE REVEREND MARION SHUTTER
THEOLOGY FOR THE MODERN WORLD

The Reverend James Tuttle's successor, the Reverend Marion Shutter, was quite different from his predecessor, despite the fact that he had been handpicked by Tuttle.

Shutter embraced science and evolution, arguing in "The Christian Life in the Modern World" against tying one's spirituality to dogma or any theological or economic system. According to Shutter, science had no conflict with religion, and the focus rather should be on the life of Christ.

Shutter's concern was not whether Jesus was God or human, but rather what the story of Jesus meant to Universalists and the world. In "The Significance of Jesus," preached in 1939, he said, "Jesus still stands in the world as the basis of our hopes for the future." In another sermon he stated his belief that he would be with God after he died.

Any study of him, however, would be incomplete without observing his disdain for Communism, for the labor movement, and for the Roosevelt Administration's New Deal. In one sermon, "Against a Philosophy of Defeat," June 1939, he condemned a statement by Marriner Eccles, an official of the administration, who had said people were entitled to a place to live, protection against unemployment, the right to adequate medical attention, and educational opportunities. These ideas, Shutter felt, were a philosophy of defeat. The belief that one could be a victim of circumstances beyond his or her control could destroy the character of the individual. He said that it is in the individual response to circumstances by which character is formed.

The two sermon excerpts that follow were delivered in the 1930s, a period of profound change. The Great Depression was ravaging the nation, and the Democratic Administration and its New Deal were struggling to cope with it.

—*Jessica Wicks*

A handwritten copy of one of the Reverend Marion Shutter's sermons, 1936

The Significance of Jesus

This sermon was given on Easter 1939 and chosen by Shutter the day before he died as a sermon he wanted printed

In all ages Jesus has presented a problem to be solved instead of a life to be lived. The ordinary discussions about Jesus try to prove that he was God or at least some supernatural being. . . . I am not going to try to find out how much of him was God and how much of him was man. . . . The Trinity and his relation to it are questions of abstract theological mathematics, and have no more to do with the conduct of life than Einstein's theory of relativity. What I am concerned with today is not what Jesus meant to another generation. . . . The question is: "what does he mean today?" He looked ahead and believed that something of him was going to survive, that his words at least would live, though earth and heaven passed. But something more than that. The influence of Jesus in the world now and always is the influence of a great personality. . . . Jesus is still the head of a mighty enterprise. This man dared to dream of a moral conquest of the world. He dared to make it the one purpose of his life.

The Pillars of the Temple

Our civilization . . . has its defects. If you doubt it, read the doleful articles written about it. . . . Fifty theorists want you to try their particular adventures in cloud-land. If the capitalistic system . . . must go, so be it. But remember that it is the system under which the individual and society have made the greatest strides in human history. . . . Under it . . . the wealth has been produced . . . which is in the process of redistribution. . . . We have just recognized [the Soviet Union] and given her a status of respectability. And in gratitude for all this, Russia now proposes to buy all of our goods that we will lend her the money to pay for! . . . We have created another debtor and laid another burden upon our own taxpayers, in the interest of "world prosperity!" . . . And this question of liberty is one that we are balancing in our own minds today. Some of the plans for that national recovery for which we all hope and for which we shall all work, raise the general question, How far is it necessary to bind the strong in order to help the weak? Or how far will making the strong weak help to make the weak strong? How far is it necessary to put the industries of this country under the direction of those who do not understand them, in order to secure "social justice?" I do not suggest these questions in anything but the most kindly spirit. But they are questions that are being asked.

From the shores of Buzzard's Bay they showed me years ago huge rocks projecting far out that were covered with barnacles, and they related a story of three young men whose pleasure boat had capsized and who clung to those barnacled rocks that afforded no help, but lacerated their clinging hands until the black waves swept them down. Thus does the rock of an ultra conservatism gather barnacles that cut the hands clinging for help until the black waves of utter negation and unbelief sweep appealing souls into the abyss. But the rock, after all, is not immovable, is not impregnable. . . . So whatever rock obstructs the highways of God's new thought and life shall be shaken and shattered by the still stronger forces of reason and of love, that the chariot of Jehovah may sweep forward on its restless course.
—the Reverend Marion Shutter, 1907

The Reverend Carl Olson
Inclusive Universalist

The Reverend Carl Olson was encouraged to come west following the Reverend Marion Shutter's death in 1939 by the general superintendent of the Universalist Church of America, the Reverend Robert Cummins.

Olson shared Cummins' view of an uncircumscribed Universalism, and his inclusive message reinvigorated the congregation from the shrunken group of about 40 members to a congregation of 450 adults and 600 children by the time of his retirement in 1963.

The theological content of Olson's sermons is reflective of the focus and vision of sermons in the early twenty-first century. He put more emphasis on the Bible—there are references to "today's Scripture reading," and some might disagree with his views on immortality. But the essential message was one of love and hope and an inclusive religion that "holds that every person not only has the right and the privilege, but also bears the burden and the responsibility of thinking honestly, of examining carefully, of speaking in accordance with his convictions."

His style was scholarly and lucid, and he usually emphasized that his views were not dogmatic. But he could also wax indignant when the subject was St. Augustine or Billy Graham.

Olson's sermons were preserved in the church archives in the form of pamphlets, financed by the printing fund of the Association of Universalist Women (AUW), some with printings as large as 5,000 copies.

—John Addington

The future of religion, as it seems to me, is to be found within the essential being of him who can understand that: From the day of his birth a man reaches out, first with his hands, then with his mind, never satisfied, until at last he reaches out with his heart.
—the Reverend Carl Olson, "The Future of Religion," 1961

On Immortality

My basic conviction is of my own ignorance. I do not know what lies ahead. Beyond this, I admit a mild curiosity. But I am enjoying this life sufficiently not to want to satisfy the curiosity immediately. . . . Yet there is one aspect of my own attitude which seems to be understandably individualistic: it would be reasonable and satisfactory to me if, in the economy of the universe, my energies and substance should support one flower of the earth in time to come. . . . It seems to me that none of us could wish for more than this: that our lives should be built through the years that they deserve continuance. And it would not surprise me, if this were true, that it should come to pass.

An Understanding of Liberal Religion

- Religious liberalism teaches not merely that Jesus was human, not divine, but that the human race is capable of producing such leaders as Jesus, as Buddha, Confucius and others, and it teaches that all men are the sons of God, actually or potentially.
- Religious liberalism teaches that men love and yearn for good. They make mistakes in the efforts to attain good, as do we all, but they—and we—continue to seek it. Children are born, not of or in sin, but of their parents' love of life and desire for fulfillment.
- Religious liberalism teaches that the religious books of all peoples are to be respected and revered as the products of the aspirations and as their interpretations of the meaning of life.
- Religious liberalism teaches that life is unending, that death is a phase of life, that the forces of life are present everywhere, at work constantly, neither beginning nor ending ever, at any point in time, as far as we know.
- And as for belief in a personal God, religious liberalism knows that all so-called personal Gods are determined by the ideals of men, in different ages, in different places, at different stages of growth. They change as man changes. We respect these human ideals and human yearnings, but we do not deify them. We try to reach outward and beyond.
- Religious liberalism holds that every person not only has the right and the privilege, but also bears the burden and the responsibility of thinking honestly, of examining carefully, of speaking in accordance with his convictions. Each individual is morally bound to think what he MUST think in the light of his own experience and understanding. It is the duty of each parent and teacher to free the child to accept, to understand, and to live in accordance with his universal human responsibility and privilege.

The capacity for getting along with our neighbor depends to a large extent on the capacity for getting along with ourselves. Self-righteousness is a manifestation of self-contempt.

Blind faith is to a considerable extent a substitute for the lost faith in ourselves. Insatiable desire is often a substitute for hope. Accumulation is frequently a substitute for growth. Fervent hustling is sometimes a substitute for purposeful action. Pride, perhaps, becomes a substitute for unattainable self-respect. And a preoccupation with immortality is, per chance, an admission of a worthless life.
—the Reverend Carl Olson, "The Larger Faith"

THE REVEREND JOHN CUMMINS
ELOQUENT VISIONARY

John Cummins was born just three weeks after his father was ordained as a Universalist minister. The Reverend Robert Cummins went on to be the vibrant leader of the Universalist denomination. Growing up in that intellectual household well-prepared young John Cummins for a ministry that was both activist and visionary.

His ministry at First Universalist began in 1963, the year President John F. Kennedy was assassinated, the Vietnam War was heating up, and the Civil Rights movement was in full swing. Cummins marched in Selma, provided counseling for conscientious objectors, and, after the congregation declared First Universalist a sanctuary church in 1984, wrote a commentary in the *Minneapolis Star Tribune*, saying, "Sanctuary is the heart and soul of all high religion and of civilization itself."

He occasionally took a Biblical passage or story as a basis for his sermons, but often turned to more contemporary historical figures or early Universalists, *way-showers* he called them: Jesus and the Buddha, Gandhi and King, prophets who offered ethical and moral guidance as well as spiritual inspiration. A Cummins sermon could focus on historical Universalists, on contemporary life, on a major issue of the day, on censorship and human rights, on peace and justice. The sermons were thoughtful, well-researched and, above all, direct and eloquent. More than once he reminded the congregation that if you want to know what you believe, you simply need to look at your checkbook and see where you spend. He often challenged popular assumptions, pointing out their dubious value.

He understood that change must begin at home. In a sermon preached in 1974, he pointed out that "In the directory of the . . . [UUA] for 1973, there are only 30 women listed as ministers. . . . Will the day EVER come, I sometimes wonder, when a major Unitarian Universalist church in a major city will seek out and . . . employ a woman as their minister?"

—*Kathy Coskran*

I have never believed in a hereafter. What I do believe is that each person born into the world is totally unique, a new creation, a fresh and radiant possibility. I further believe in the immortality of influence . . . that each life makes a contribution that is totally unique, and which only that person can make, which becomes a part of the ongoing stream of life. I believe that our mistakes and weaknesses die with us, but that our victories of kindness and character remain to bless humanity forever.
—the Reverend John Cummins

Message to Future Generations
from the introduction to his book of sermons, *This Strange and Wondrous Journey*

What I would like to say to the people of the future is this: You will look back on us with astonishment at the truths that stared us in the face, and which we did not see. You will look with wonder at the bright toys, which we created, and used only for the rape of the planet, and one another. It will seem strange and beyond believing that we reached for the stars, and did not know the simplest keys for living well together.

But know this also, you of the future, you with your libraries and fountains, you in your star cities. Know that even in our slumbers we dreamed. In our fumbling, shadowed search for mistaken glories, even in our clumsy cruelties, it was for you that we dreamed. Beneath the piled up centuries, below the lost and ruined rubble of our striving, it was you who lay safe-enfolded in the womb of our dreaming: you, the first cause of all our daring. Even now it comforts me to know that it shall be one day as the Way Showers have for centuries foretold.

In that far age and in the chrysalis of time, it shall be your glory and a cause of pride that, born into a universe without justice or mercy, our kind bethought itself of justice and mercy, and put them there. Remember us for this.

Sanctuary

What we would do as a congregation in granting sanctuary to a Salvadoran might well, as the law is now being interpreted, a felony —a punishable act, even the legal defense of which could be costly. There comes a time, however, when religious people must do what their religious conscience tells them they must do. It is the moment of truth when they must pay the price if they would own their own souls, lest that which they profess and the church itself become a hollow mockery. Religion has stood against the cruelty of the secular world many times in many places, and for many centuries, and will again, I am sure. And whenever it has done so, the world itself has become both more human, and more divine.

Prayer is what you wish, want and hope for more than anything else in the world, the deepest desire of your soul. . . . It is wise and healthful for us human beings to take regular moments . . . to reflect and bring to the surface in our conscious minds just what our deepest desires may be. In the end, however, prayer is action, for no one who has a truly held desire or belief fails to act upon it. . . . Hidden from view in the school prayer issue is the pernicious idea that those who don't pray in accepted manner are really responsible for all America's problems— immorality, drug use, crime, and the breakup of homes as we have known them, not to mention "secular humanism," atheism and anti-religion.
—the Reverend John Cummins, "God, Prayer and the Public Schools," 1982

THE REVERENDS SUSAN MILNOR AND TERRY SWEETSER FROM THE PERSONAL TO THE COSMIC

Only 14 years after the Reverend John Cummins wondered aloud if a major Unitarian Universalist congregation would call a woman minister, First Universalist had a woman minister in a senior position and its first co-ministry when the congregation called the Reverends Susan Milnor and Terry Sweetser in 1988.

On their first Sunday, May 9, 1988, Sweetser delivered the sermon at 9:30 a.m., "Screaming with Laughter" and Milnor at 11 a.m., "Telling Stories." The two sermons were a prophetic introduction to the style and theology of the co-ministry. Sweetser quoted literary scholar Northrup Frye regarding the essential elements of the comic story: perilous journey, hard struggle, unexpected, but fought for success. Milnor spoke of stories in the interpretive sense: how what we perceive as our personal story is essential and definitive in determining the truth and religious scope of our lives. They both often used stories and the language of struggle in their sermons, making the congregation laugh and cry, as they described relationships that everybody struggled with—with parents, with children, with partners, with life.

Sweetser came from a long line of Universalists and preached an optimistic theology of hope and possibility realized through action. Milnor described herself as an "almost pessimist"—a realist—whose deeply felt, personal sermons resonated with the congregation. Theirs was an energetic, activist ministry, that built on the social justice programs well established in the Cummins' years and attracted so many new members that they were soon holding three services every Sunday morning.

The lovely benediction they introduced perhaps best encapsulates their theology and ministry: *let us be about the task*. Much of their theology focused on what one can do today that will bear fruit in the future, both locally and globally.

—*Kathy Coskran*

These words served as inspiration for a benediction introduced by the Reverends Sweetser and Milnor:

Each of us is an artist whose task it is to shape life into some semblance of the pattern we dream about. The molding is not of self alone, but of shared tomorrows and times we shall never see.
So let us be about the task. The materials are very precious and they are perishable.
—the Reverend Arthur Graham

Susan Milnor: On Dreaming Together
sermon delivered hours before the congregational vote to buy the Dupont building

I sometimes worry, when we talk about our future, that we talk about it just with our heads. Yet when we talk about moving from this building to another, we are talking about something with deep emotional and spiritual implications. When we talk about moving we are talking about leaving a home. And that's something that affects all of us who care about our community. . . . For some people, grief isn't the issue: fear is. There are many fears associated with both moving and staying. When it comes to moving, some people have fears about the safety of the [new] neighborhood, or our ability to bear the cost, or the amount of growth or change we will experience. . . . When it comes to staying, some people fear our volunteers, staff and ministers will burn out and leave under the stressful circumstances . . . or that we will become even more divorced from the most urgent problems and issues of Minneapolis than we already are. . . . Regardless of the way you choose to vote . . . we need to acknowledge the deepest truth of all [that] . . . the real cradle of our dreams is the bond between us, the vision of life that holds us together and molds us into a people.

Beauty Before Us

If you look back at all the horrible things that happened following Columbus's voyages, especially the aggressive, cruel acts, one tragic flaw sits at the center of them all. That is people's inability to see the gifts and talents, the wisdom, the accomplishments of people who talk differently, who love differently, who name the sacred differently. When Columbus came to the West, he found 300 functioning societies, with governmental structure, language, history, religion and art. Yet in 1537, nearly fifty years later, Pope Paul III hoped to settle a controversy when he declared the natives to be human. People could not see the beauty before them. And still we struggle with that. Whether it is racism in our cities or prejudice in our schools, we struggle with it. No, we are not responsible for the sins of our fathers and mothers. But we are accountable for whether we continue their legacy. . . . We are accountable for whether the world's rain forests, which serve as home and the source of life to 50 million indigenous people, survive . . . we are responsible for whether the rights of Native Americans are finally respected. We are accountable for whether we see the beauty before us. And spiritually, we have the opportunity to repent . . . By repent I mean not to drown in guilt or shame . . . but rather, to dedicate ourselves to doing things differently.

The answer to death is life. It's treating every bit of it as precious and worthy. It's glimpsing the galaxies, yes, but it's also taking the risk to love, because if love is what you're after, love is what you give. The answer is celebrating life, dancing right along in the parade of images that hint at what is beautiful and good and ultimate.
—the Reverend Susan Milnor

In a 1992 sermon, "As Thyself," the Reverend Terry Sweetser told of a disastrous attempt to help a troubled friend, Stuart, who told him, "All I needed was to talk to an old friend. You know, to share my pain. I don't need to be fixed up. I just needed to talk to someone. . . . Go home."

Sometime later, Sweetser said, he read the story of the Good Samaritan. "A light was beginning to dawn on me. . . . If I had really appreciated what Jesus was saying, I would have realized Stuart was a different person, not just an extension of myself. I would have known that to love him as self, I had to try to understand and address his needs.

"A couple of years later, I called to apologize. . . . 'Terry, he said, 'sometimes you act as if you are in charge of the world. But at least you go on trying to learn from it.'

Terry Sweetser: Thriving in the Waiting Room

What our children teach us about creativity is that life's waiting room is really a playground if we persist in having a perspective of playfulness. Do I mean that life is all fun and games? Not at all. Like most of you, I have encountered enough pain and loss . . . to know that enduring is sometimes a challenge in itself. From finding my mother after she took her own life to realizing that my own pain had made me dependent on alcohol, I have seen that life can beat us down . . . To live radiantly, we must be willing to turn our pain and problems upside down and look at them anew; we must be willing to move, somehow, beyond all the prescriptions for living, all the 'shoulds' and 'oughts' that are supposed to make us whole but don't, and be willing to reinvent ourselves.

Why Things Go Right

Universalism is an optimistic religion. Unlike many faiths that suggest we humans are helpless in the hands of an angry God, Universalism suggests we may be liberated to the fullness of life by putting faith in our ability to always find positive possibilities. That means as religious people our spiritual discipline involves learning to edit our experiences for hope and rehearsing our futures for liberation from helplessness. A vital part of our spiritual journey is to cultivate habits that confront a sense of inevitable doom, permanent pain, and senseless self-shame. A cultivation of wonder and awe are also part of the spiritual journey, but these are hard to find if you feel helpless much of the time.

Appreciation of Diversity

Ours is a faith which must move beyond tolerance to appreciation of diverse spiritual positions. Therefore I dislike theological labels. Like Hans Kung [a liberal Catholic theologian], I am a humanist who believes human beings can do the work of making the world a hospitable place in which to live. Like Frederick May Eliot [a Unitarian leader], I am a naturalistic theist who is confident that there is enough mystery in a snowflake to prove gracious divinity. Like my great-uncle Henry Chapin Sweetser, former superintendent of the American Universalist Convention, I pursue a religious path informed by the radical teachings of Jesus. Above all, though, I have given my heart to what [a friend and mentor] calls 'a search for the transcendent center of value and power which binds us together in loyalty and trust.' I give myself over to that search and also to the belief that in the company of this congregation, I can find that center time and time again.

The Reverend Gretchen Thompson: Associate Minister of Community

The Reverend Gretchen Thompson served First Universalist Church as Associate Minister of Community in 1994 and 1995. A hallmark of her sermons was her inclusivity. In the summer of 1994 she preached about diversity issues, positing the inherent right of every human being to name his or her own self, asserting that no outside individual or institution ought dare to do it.

She wished aloud that the congregation create a "Welcome Here Cookbook" in which everybody would submit recipes dear to their hearts and reflective of their own life stories, and that each person would then be categorized through the cookbook as salads, entrees, souffles, desserts and so forth. Her humorous suggestion became a 160-page cookbook, *The Welcome Here Cookbook,* in which the congregation revealed themselves as soups and muffins, main dishes and puddings, emblematic of Thompson's gift for bringing a community together.

Slow Miracles

Slow miracles are, on a day to day basis, almost invisible. In fact, one slow miracle can arch like a rainbow, completely ethereal, over years and years.

Referring to Unity House, Thompson said, "They got a house right smack in the middle of the needy neighborhood and sent *friendly visitors* out into the surrounding streets to listen to what the people were saying. Based on what they heard, they'd create ministries opening the doors of their house to everyone in welcome. . . . They taught classes in English and U.S. history and established clubs for boys, girls, and mothers. The Mothers' Club gained a vibrancy of its own when the mothers themselves began organizing playgrounds. There followed a full gymnasium and men's and women's sports teams.

"This little house continued to be a powerful and healing presence in that neighborhood for over 50 years. . . . I believe that our corporate story is a slow miracle, a rainbow which arches in time through the history of this city. . . . And so it does. And so may it continue, more vibrant than ever."

It's not too early to picture ourselves swinging open our doors again to the neighborhood and giving all kinds of folks welcome, to imagine our newly mounted sign, or the interior space renovated to be friendly and strong and true, equipped for the ministries we have chosen. It is not too early to imagine that miracle unfolding. Indeed, I see it through the eyes of my own faith as if it were already there.
—the Reverend Gretchen Thompson

THE REVEREND FRANK RIVAS
REV.ELATIONS

Our story does not end with having found a spiritual home. Now that we've found our home, the real story begins—the story of trusting one another enough to take off the masks, the story of loving one another enough to see through the demons, the story of listening to one another enough to forge a new way of being in community, the story of being faithful enough to do the work of justice, to do the work of mercy, and to walk humbly with our God.
—the Reverend Frank Rivas, 2005

The Reverend Frank Rivas introduced the Buddhist gong to the worship service—a singing bowl struck three times to call the congregation to silence, to worship, to being present and centered together every Sunday morning. The sound of that gong—beauty and spirit, bell song and space between the song—was emblematic of the gifts he brought to First Universalist Church.

Rivas chose *Rev.Elations* as the title of his monthly *Liberal* column because he was about both revelation—removing the veil from the holy—and elation—being alive to the wonder of the world.

His sermons came from a structured outline rather than a printed text because he wasn't comfortable simply reading something he had written. He wanted to be responsive to the people in the pews, to say more if the congregation didn't yet comprehend, to say less if he saw he had said enough. A Rivas sermon was not a performance, nor a conversation, but an unfolding exchange, a discovery and revelation for both speaker and listener.

Rivas cared deeply about the church, and through nearly 10 years of his shared ministry, the congregation was served by a graceful man, a serious man who didn't take himself too seriously. Humor came naturally to him, to ease a difficult situation or simply to acknowledge the presence of the absurd. His ministry and his theology were like the strokes of the bell: direct and simple, embracing both the sound and the silence.

—*Kathy Coskran*

On the Religious Life

The Zen Buddhist tea ceremony is wordless, elegant in its simplicity. . . . I've participated in the ceremony but . . . this ceremony will never mean the same thing to me that it means to the Japanese. For them, sitting on the floor and drinking green tea out of cups without handles is the most ordinary of activities. For me . . . it will always be foreign and exotic. If I were to practice the ceremony . . . as an American, I would call myself to awareness as the water heats over my stove, as I grind coffee, and as I pour water over the coffee, through the paper filter, into a cup with handle. Then I would practice what Zen teaches, that awareness of the most ordinary activities is all we need to become whole.

The goal of the religious life is not to form an intellectual rigorous theology. Nor is it to use the most correct name for the Holy, nor even to name the Holy, as Moses discovered when he encountered the burning bush. The goal of the religious life is to transform ourselves into people of justice, of compassion, of humility. What is required of us but that we do justice, love mercy, and walk humbly with our God? The goal of the religious life, as Universalist Clinton Lee Scott wrote in the 1940s, is found "in the fount of common everyday life. . . . Not in formal observances, not in creeds or doctrines, however long ago proclaimed, but the lives we live, in the home, in the community, and in the world, are the religious ways of life to be found. A religious person is one who fulfills his [or her] highest function as a human being in relation with other persons.

On Finding Love

"Love should grow like a wild iris in the fields," [from a Susan Griffin poem], but never does. We imagine, each of us, that if our conditions were better, if we had better parents and a better education, if we hadn't let the perfect spouse get away or had landed the perfect job, then we would grow into the wholeness of our being, into the wholeness of our love.

I know this because I too have felt crippled in my own growth toward love, and I too have blamed the continuing imperfection of life. However, it may just be that love grows best in the messiness of our lives, amid losses and frustrations, in the kitchens and the dinner hour, in the social hall after the service—with our competing agendas and children, wanting to go home, tugging at their parents.

If what is required of us is justice, compassion, and humility, then we ought to be careful about criticizing how others worship and pray. A group of convicts and addicts who hold hands and pray that each would feel the love of the others, who respond with "Yes, Lord, yes," who call one another to turn their lives toward God . . . far from deserving our criticism, these men model the values of our tradition.

—the Reverend Frank Rivas, 2005

THE REVEREND KATE TUCKER
TRANSFORMATIVE RELATIONSHIPS

The Reverend Kate Tucker's welcoming spirit and gift for inclusiveness endeared her to the congregation from the start of her ministry at First Universalist in 1997. The most public aspect of her theological viewpoint is present in her sermons, but the transformative aspects of her ministry happened behind the scenes. A deeply spiritual person who practices personal meditation, Tucker touched the spiritual hunger of the congregation and provided a variety of ways for fellow searchers to deepen and enrich their own spiritual lives through the development of pastoral care programs, in the creation of Welcome Home Wednesday, in a small group ministry called Sharing Circles, and in a contemplative practices group.

Tucker is a captivating preacher who draws on ancient texts and contemporary poetry for inspiration; her radiant presence in the pulpit communicates as much as her well-chosen words. She can be present to a single individual or to a sanctuary crammed to capacity, with a genuineness born from her own humble quest for the holy and from a generosity that welcomes the first time visitor and the oldest member.

We are a community of faith drawn together not by doctrine, but by our desire to be a people of open minds, open hearts, and open hands. We seek to live lives of integrity, in grateful relationship with one another and with that sustaining, transforming power many call God and we often call Love.
—the Reverend Kate Tucker

She believes in questions, values the question, knows how to live the question and asks questions because she knows the answers will shift or open to something new. Hers is a theology of the possible, of hope, of tomorrow. Early in her sermon, "The Question of Questions," she said, "I am always suspicious of people who are certain about the answer to a problem in living but who clearly have not thought deeply about the various ways of formulating the question."

She closed with "How is it that simply *asking* a question can bring about a healing? We are a fellowship of learners, a company of seekers—and sometimes what we seek, we find. May we be patient toward all that is unsolved in our hearts, and thankful for each and everything that's solved."

Perhaps that is her secret—patience and faith in the power of the question, an openness to seeking, and a trust in what comes next.

—*Kathy Coskran*

Oh Child, Oh Child

Unless you turn and become as children you cannot enter the realm of God.

I don't think that saying is telling us to go back in time or become irresponsible. I think it's telling us to look into our hearts and read the truth that surely is still written there. The truth that we were once part of the mingled vastness of the universe, and we will be again. And while we're here, between one vastness and the other, we *are* like children: Dependent on the bounty of the earth and the kindness of others. Wearing, on the outside, these unstable, changing, replaceable bodies. Wearing, on the inside, a mysterious strength that no one can name for us, and that can't be bought or sold.

Authorities Disagree

The Christmas story is a love story of cosmic size, about love between human beings and their one source, the spirit of life. I knew that as a child. That was the magic of Christmas—the promise that the impossible good thing would arrive, the anticipation, the music so full of calm and joy, the surprise when it was all true. I knew it then, and it made me dizzy and dancey.

Christmas was a cosmic chick flick, a you've got mail, a pride and prejudice where after all the waiting and agonized pacing between hope and despair, the gift comes, and the truth is revealed, which is:

The universe knows, the Great Spirit cares.
The reality at the core of life loves us back.
The word is made flesh. You've got mail.

Universalists long lived by this love story, letting it feed their justice efforts, and guide their lives in community. No wonder it's often hard to put our faith into words. Our mission, we say is to spread the Universalist message of love and hope.

What we're saying is: We are lovers. We're basically lovers. No wonder it's hard to say more. And though we keep trying, all the while we know—the only thing is to live it.

I've come to see all our rituals as marriage ceremonies. In our rituals, we marry time to eternity. We marry the ordinary stuff of our daily lives—the flour and the yeast and the water—to the one great human drama, the one timeless and epic journey. We are leavened into that one loaf. The dough rises and has a life of its own. The sourness changes to fragrance. Heroes are transformed and released into themselves. Bread becomes more than bread, and it feeds us all.
—the Reverend Kate Tucker

THIS WE BELIEVE
STATEMENTS FROM MEMBERS

Ultimately, coming back and working with the history of this phenomenal church the past three years in preparation for the celebration of our sesquicentennial has been such an inspiring, educational and satisfying experience and reminds me why I became a member over 30 years ago.
Carol Jackson, remarks made in 2009

When someone asks me what UUism is, I'll continue to say it's the coolest religion ever.
Adrian Wackett, Coming of Age Spiritual Statement, 2007

In college it was easy to find someone to chat with about what I believe, challenging and learning from each other. As an adult I need that kind of spiritually open community and I find it here at First Universalist.
Shannon Dahmes, member since 2001

We came to First Universalist for our children and stayed for the community.
Nora Whiteman, member since 1992

Gwen and I became Unitarian Universalists because we believe only universality can encompass the butterfly and the tiger, and only tolerance can give dimension to the walls of the mind. We found joy in its concept of linkage, hope in its cadence, strength in its doubts. We wanted to pulsate with that wondrous, vaporous aura that celebrates a diversity ever reseeding the world.
Preben Mosborg, remarks made in 1992

The most important thing about this church, to me, are the people I love. To sit in the midst of friends on a Sunday morning, to know that we share the same basic attitudes and values, to gain courage and strength from their friendship, to know them as hilarious companions as well as rescuers in a storm. . . . This church is like home to me . . . and is a kind of link to greatness, and goodness, and courage, and love beyond all understanding.
Grace Wilson, remarks made 50 years after she became a member in 1942

Looking back over my past life and career in this city of my adoption I feel that nothing has added more to my well being and genuine satisfaction than my fifty years' connection with the Church of the Redeemer.
William D. Washburn, founding member, remarks made 50 years later in 1909

When the benediction was pronounced, the congregation did not all immediately rush pell-mell for the door, in an evident made rush to get to dinner. But a large number stopped to salute their nearest neighbors in the pews at least, and perhaps some of them would slap each other on the back to emphasize the heartiness of the salutation.
Honorable William P. Roberts, describing his first service at First Universalist Society in 1874

BY OUR DEEDS

Children served by First Universalist's Unity House nursery

May this spiritual community and the love that surrounds us provide the courage we need to say yes—to say yes when called to fight for liberty and justice for all, and yes to honoring the past by investing in the future. Abraham [Lincoln] and Martin [Luther King, Jr.] are gone, but John and Dru [Cummins] and all of us are still here working for a more perfect Union, for a more just world, for today, and for times we shall never see.

—First Universalist member and Minnesota Secretary of State Mark Ritchie, in "Abraham, Martin, John and Dru," a sermon delivered January 2008

THE GREAT QUESTIONS

Unity Summer interns in action

The Reverend Marion Shutter, in his address at the 50th Anniversary Celebration, observed that a modern church, centrally located, such as Church of the Redeemer, "should be open more than one day in a week and should furnish a rallying-place for the people socially and for their work . . . ." He went on to describe the role of the church in the life of the community.

"The great questions by which any church must be judged are: What have its ideas and ideals done for the community? What kind of men and women has it produced? And what has been the character of their deeds?"

These are indeed the great questions, for by our deeds we shall be known. As the previous chapters have shown, First Universalist Church, its members and its ministers were central to the growth and development of Minneapolis. Community outreach, helping others, creating institutions that served the present and prepared for the future came naturally to the early Universalists and have continued for 150 years.

This section, *By Our Deeds,* highlights the multiple levels of service the church and its members have offered to others. We have cared for each other when we were sick or suffering; we have cared for our neighbors who were cold or hungry or scared; we have spoken out for justice and equality and demonstrated for peace; we have worked together for the health of our planet, for mother earth. We know, as Margaret Mead wrote, to "never doubt that a small group of thoughtful, committed citizens can change the world; indeed, it's the only thing that ever has."

An Act of Love: Caring For Each Other

If tempted to believe that the present generation originated the concept of pastoral care at First Universalist Church, reading from the minutes of the Ladies Social Circle from the early 1900s will indicate otherwise.

Annual Flower Mission Report, 1910
Flowers have been sent to 60 people during the year, and to the hospital 12 times.

May 21, 1913
Using money out of the Eastman Fund for the flowers used for church decorations, which were sent to sick members and shut-ins . . . was earnestly discussed by many ladies present. As this is an act of love . . . motion carried.

Dec. 9, 1914
The aid committee reported having sent a ton of coal to a needy woman.

During the Reverend Carl Olson's ministry in the 1940s and 1950s, the women's group continued providing flowers to members who were sick or shut in through its Flower Committee. The minister visited members in need. In 1943 he made 288 parish calls, and he ensured that newsletters and letters were sent to those in military service, with whom he also corresponded personally. In 1947 the church sponsored a blood bank for the first time. By 1951, the church newsletter included a column about members, and the news included illnesses.

By 1963, after the Reverend John Cummins arrived, member Grace Wilson led volunteer efforts to help church families who were grieving or in need. The church published a small pamphlet, "How You Help Others," to give examples of ways to minister to those grieving. Cummins made house calls, and he asked certain members to assist him in visiting those suffering or in crisis.

After the Reverends Terry Sweetser and Susan Milnor arrived as co-ministers in 1988, the church grew so rapidly that the ministers had difficulty responding to the many pastoral care needs. Milnor was instrumental in the formation of the Pastoral Care Council, which

Dorothy Mooney, Nell McClure and Margit Berg, circa 1990, at the Caring Corner of 5000 Girard Avenue South

Arlene Jacobson started the Caring Corner, which provides cards for members to send to those needing comfort, and served as the pastoral care director on the All Church Council for many years. Members Julie Howard, Margit Berg (above), Ruth Arnold, Cassi Neff and Carolyn and Bob Moe, and Sue Schiess also have played pivotal roles in our tending to the special needs of congregants.

In 1999 First Universalist joined the TRUST consortium of south Minneapolis churches. TRUST, which had begun in 1973 as a Christian group to provide community services, had broadened to serve other denominations. The Board of Trustees was persuaded to take a special collection so that the church could contribute to TRUST. First Universalist members were soon involved in TRUST activities, especially the visiting nurse program. For the 2008-09 church year First Universalist contributed $6,000 to TRUST.

systemized the tradition of sending cards to church members. A Memorial Services Committee was formed, and the Befrienders program was begun with the help of an extensive training program through the Wilder Foundation.

In 1997, the Reverend Kate Tucker called a meeting of former pastoral care volunteers to discuss ways to energize a new committee and composed a list of potential helpers. Sue Schiess turned down a position on the board in order to lead the pastoral care committee.

In December 2000, a crisis in a church family galvanized the congregation to support the pastoral care cause. The family's Christmas tree caught fire, the father was critically burned, and the family home was destroyed. The church held a blood drive, which was then renewed at First Universalist as an annual event. According to Schiess, "Our deeply felt need to help the family—and our subsequently proven ability to do it well—changed how we saw ourselves as a congregation."

The circular bond of pastoral care continued and grew stronger. By 2009, pastoral care involved nearly 200 volunteers yearly, more than 20 percent of the church membership. Volunteers served in a variety of ways, including helping at memorial services and receptions, knitting comfort shawls, making and delivering care baskets, visiting and delivering flowers to those ill or shut-in, making and delivering meals to those in need, providing rides to medical appointments, and hosting a blood bank and a flu-shot clinic.

—*Mary Junge*

Sue Schiess, who received a Comfort Shawl after breaking her neck

Comfort Shawls

My Comfort Shawl was the all-around hug that was otherwise physically impossible during the three months of my confinement. All of the support I received from the congregation (cards, meals, flowers) were like a giant psychic hug, but my shawl provided a physical manifestation of that support. Every night at bedtime, I would position the shawl across the top of my recliner (sleeping in a bed was not possible). I'd pull up a blanket, which could only reach my armpits because of the "halo" supporting my head and neck. Then I'd reach back over my shoulders, find the soft, cozy shawl with my fingertips, and I'd pull it around my shoulders. It felt like a prayer—a blessing—a very warm hug.

By Our Deeds

THE ASSOCIATION OF UNIVERSALIST WOMEN: A CENTURY OF ACTIVISM AND EMPOWERMENT

What church has ever had a nobler band of women looking after and advancing its interests than the Church of the Redeemer has had!
— the Reverend James Tuttle in *Universalism in Minneapolis*

First Universalist was a place where women knew they could have an influential role in addition to being worker bees. It is no secret that women cooked the food, cleaned the kitchen, taught Sunday school, volunteered for memorial services, and visited the sick and the needy. They also organized and worked and agitated for social change in many different ways. Perhaps the most powerful was through the Association of Universalist Women (AUW) that was incorporated in 1907. It took more than a hundred years for a woman to chair the church Board of Trustees—Myrna Hansen in 1967, noted as Mrs. Charles F. Hansen in the records—so creating a separate organization with its own board and budget was necessary even in the liberal church.

From the beginning the AUW was rooted in charity and social reform work. The AUW hosted Christmas parties for the mothers and children from Unity House; they sent Christmas gifts to charity workers in Japan and toys to an orphanage in Greece. In the 1950s, members folded their dollars into the pockets of paper baseballs, placed them on a tree at their annual tea, and donated the money to a cause.

The charity work was important, but it was through involvement in national issues that the AUW members found their voice, both individually and collectively. The women's suffrage movement, the feminist and civil rights movements, the landmark abortion rights case Roe v. Wade, the Equal Rights Amendment, and the gay rights movement empowered women to speak out and speak up. Clara Barton spoke at the Church of the Redeemer, as did AUW member Mary Garard Andrews, who was also an officer of the National Suffrage Association. The AUW worked to get the vote for women in the early

The Red Cross bandage-rolling team of First Universalist in 1945. Longtime member Grace Wilson (1909-1992) said that her mother, Mrs. Edward Scofield (pictured above seated front left), joined the Universalist church after seeing a pregnant woman singing in the choir at Tuttle Church, a radical act in the early twentieth century.

Dru Cummins made a huge impact on First Universalist, and the denomination, after she and husband, the Reverend John Cummins, arrived in Minneapolis in 1963.

Drusilla Cummins (1925-)

Drusilla (Dru) Cummins went to the Unitarian Universalist (UUA) General Assembly in Philadelphia in 1974 to ask for space so she and her UU Women's Federation (UUWF) cohorts could present the first Ministry to Women Award, but they were refused because they were an auxiliary organization. Undeterred, Cummins and others called a press conference, then rented a nearby church along with 55 buses to take women there, so they could present the first Ministry to Women Award to *Ms. Magazine* editors Gloria Steinem and Pat Carbine. The award came full circle when Cummins was given the award by the UUWF in 2000.

In an essay for her alma mater, Mount Holyoke, Cummins wrote: *The stained glass ceiling had cracked, and in rapid succession I was elected trustee of the Unitarian Universalist Association, second vice moderator, first vice moderator, and chair of several committees. These positions also gave me opportunities to empower other women. I later served as the first woman chair of the board of our graduate theological school at the University of Chicago, Meadville Lombard, and I led a campaign to elect the first woman president of our denomination. I had been empowered by our liberating faith, and by women and men who share that faith.*

In 2004 the AUW honored Betty Benjamin, Dru Cummins and Sharon Bishop with an engraved plaque at the Unitarian Universalist Association's Washington Office for Advocacy and also provided funds for the Clara Barton Internship for Women's Issues to train tomorrow's leaders.

twentieth century, and in 2004 were again working for equal voting rights for all.

The feminist movement was just beginning when Dru Cummins came to First Universalist with her husband, the Reverend John Cummins. By 1970, she had become actively involved in the Unitarian Universalist Women's Federation (UUWF), the national women's organization that called for inclusive language and equal participation by women in the denomination. While president of the UUWF, Cummins appointed Sharon Bishop as the UUWF representative for the Equal Rights Amendment and Betty Benjamin as the UUWF representative for the repeal of abortion laws. Both Bishop and Benjamin were active AUW members.

Each of these three powerful women inspired other AUW women over subsequent decades and had a profound impact on the causes for which they worked, as well as on the church, the community, and the world. When 40 First Universalist women joined the march for choice in

> **Sharon Bishop (1939-2006)**
>
> Sharon Bishop became active in AUW after attending an annual tea as a guest of her mother-in-law, Frederica Bishop. After Dru Cummins appointed her as the Equal Rights Amendment (ERA) advocate for the UUWF, Sharon became the UUWF representative to the National Religious Coalition for the ERA. Sharon said, "On the one hand, it was a disappointment because the ERA amendment failed. On the other hand, it was exhilarating because we put together small committees to develop worship services and other programs for the Prairie Star District (PSD) meetings. There were always women at the meeting who hadn't connected with this kind of religion."
>
> Ritual practices were just developing at the time, and Bishop and other leaders not only tried them out, they helped to develop them. Bishop chaired and was the PSD delegate for the first Women and Religion Conference in Granville, Ohio, in 1979. In 1982 she worked with ministerial intern Laurie Bushbaum to organize the first Winter Solstice Service at First Universalist.
>
> As a nurse for the Minneapolis Public Schools, Bishop led the first in-school support groups for gay, lesbian, and transgender students in 1989. She served on a task force on gay rights under Minnesota Governor Arne Carlson, and she co-authored *Alone No More: Developing a School Support System for Gay, Lesbian, and Bisexual Youth*.
>
> — from *100 Years of Liberation: 1905-2005 Association of Universalist Women*

Sharon Bishop was generous with her time in almost every area of the church, including serving as president of the Board of Trustees from 1979 to 1981.

Washington, D.C., in 2004, the AUW board committed to developing a program for women's justice. In 2005 a subcommittee of new AUW board members, led by Betsy Allis, launched an effort to engage AUW members in developing a vision of justice and a plan to achieve that vision. As a result, the AUW board funded two campaigns: one on reproductive justice, the other on voting rights, both of which became official working groups of the Minnesota UU Social Justice Alliance (MUUSJA).

Not only did the AUW support central figures in the larger movements, it also provided a training ground for women to move into leadership roles. Many AUW events were solely for women because, in a culture

In addition to her work on reproductive rights, Betty Benjamin served on the church Board of Trustees, was president of AUW twice, and chaired the First Universalist Foundation.

Betty Benjamin (1924-2004)

Benjamin joined the fledgling movement to legalize abortion after attending a seminar on teen pregnancy at First Universalist in 1967. In 1971 she was a founding member of the Minnesota Council for the Legal Termination of Pregnancy and was president of that organization, later called NARAL Pro-Choice Minnesota, for 17 years. In 1999, on Benjamin's 75th birthday, Minnesota NARAL established a foundation in her honor to provide training for future leaders.

One week before her 80th birthday and nine weeks before her death from cancer, over 40 First Universalist members joined Benjamin, her husband Bob and a million others in Washington, D.C., for a pro-choice march.

It was at an evening church potluck discussion in January 1967 where I heard about the beginning of an organization attempting to legalize abortion. . . . The tremendous support from so many members of First Universalist has made it far easier to be in the forefront of the continuing and challenging controversy . . . Only together can we ensure freedom of choice.
— Betty Benjamin, 1992

that continued to be male-dominated, time with other women helped individuals gain strength and confidence. Women who had never led a committee meeting or spoken before a group were supported as they found their voice and their muscle. Many AUW traditions, new as well as old ones, reinforced this powerful foundation: the Holiday Tea, a tradition since 1932, and the Mother-Daughter Banquet, the Women's Spiritual Retreat, and the Women's Friendship groups are all examples of traditions that empower Universalist women individually and collectively.

Each year the AUW nominates women for the Clara Barton Sisterhood, created by the UUWF. Women aged 80 and older are first nominated by their local women's group and their names are recorded in a book kept at Federation headquarters in Boston. The AUW board members interview nominees and create a short biography for each woman nominated. Nineteen First Universalist women have been nominated for the sisterhood. Many of the biographies created for the UUWF were used for First Universalist's AUW anniversary book, *100 Years of Liberation: 1905-2005.*

—*Mary Junge*

Japanese Mission Work

The Blackmer Home for Women, founded in Tokyo, Japan, around 1902, was a place where women were taken in, cared for and provided an education. Research in First Universalist's archives housed at the Minnesota History Center suggests that the Church of the Redeemer was involved in working with that mission from its earliest days. The church was not only sending money to the Japan Endowment Fund, but participating in more direct ways.

In 1911, the sewing group was busy making kimonos for the residents of Blackmer. On May 11 of that year, there is a note that Miss Hathaway promised to visit the Women's Association before she returned to Japan. She worked in Japan, as well as in Minneapolis with Unity House.

In 1913, the Reverend Marion Shutter asked for a photo of Mrs. Patterson in Japan, where she had gone to study the mission work. In the same set of documents he also refers to home mission work among the mountain folk of North Carolina. In October of that year, church members began covering the cost of one Japanese girl per year at Blackmer.

This photograph, with only "Mrs. Ada B. Morrill" written on top, prompted a church archivist to learn more.

Notes of the Annual Report show that after Mrs. Patterson returned from Japan, she attended the meeting dressed in a Japanese costume of soft gray, complete from kimono to sandals, and spoke about the work being done at Blackmer.

In a report of the church's Committee on Business, circa 1931-32, pre-war tensions were obviously starting to rise: "Deem it advisable to restrict our missionary endeavors to satisfying our obligations of the past. We have our workers in Japan, sent there by us, and we must at least fulfill our legal responsibilities for them whether or not we approve of the actions of the Japanese government."

Archival information about the Japan and North Carolina missions is sketchy. Toward the end of the 1930s, aid to North Carolina continued, but questions were being raised about whether other pockets of poverty should be considered as well. By 1941, there was a suggestion that the Japanese men were not happy about the services provided to women, but even after the Japanese bombed Pearl Harbor, the church continued sending donations.

After World War II ended, First Universalist was involved in a new Japanese effort through the AUW, which was to send old hosiery to Japan, where women unraveled the stockings and converted them into flowers, butterflies, and other novelty items to sell.

— *Jessica Wicks*

A Welcoming Congregation

Gay Pride parade 1993

The history of First Universalist's acceptance of gay, lesbian, bisexual, and transgender members and friends is relatively recent. Precious little is documented from the early days of the church regarding gay issues. Sexual orientation was rarely discussed before 1969, when the Stonewall Rebellion in New York City largely launched the gay rights movement. It appears that there were gay church and staff members from John Cummins' time forward.

The earliest notes regarding a formal response at First Universalist to gay issues was a meeting in 1986 of the AIDS Task Force, which consisted of Sharon Bishop, Karen Bruce, John DeMars, Carol Hobart and Gail Thiele. They drafted a resolution that was forwarded to the board. On January 14, 1987, the Board of Trustees approved a resolution that included a focus on education, civil liberties, and support of those living with HIV, their families and loved ones.

Over time, First Universalist was involved in a variety of activities including educating the congregation regarding HIV, discussing safe sex, providing meeting space for two HIV support groups, and conversations on gay issues. First Wednesdays were services organized for those living with AIDS or affected by the disease. The church was one of the first in the faith community to work with the AIDS Interfaith Council of Minnesota and the Minnesota AIDS Project. Educational articles about HIV and AIDS began appearing in the *Liberal* in 1989. In 1990, letters were sent home to parents advising them of the availability of resource material for youth about HIV.

By Our Deeds

The first same-sex marriage at our church was held on Sept. 16, 1989, of Polly [Munts] and Deborah Talen (ceremony pictured above) whose second daughter Lydia (below) was dedicated in the church in 1993.

It was not all about the tragedy of AIDS, however. In the spring of 1988, partners Deborah Talen and Polly Munts joined the church, shortly before the Reverends Terry Sweetser and Susan Milnor arrived at First Universalist. They made a nervous phone call to ask if Milnor or Sweetser would consider doing a same-sex wedding. To their delight, Milnor was comfortable with the idea. They said their vows on September 16, 1989, and Munts changed her last name to Talen.

In the late 1980s, a group of women including Velma Wagner, Kit Ketchum, and Deborah Talen began a gay/lesbian/bisexual/transgender (GLBT) committee at the church. Around the same time, the Unitarian Universalist Association (UUA) began a program for congregations that sought to become more inclusive. The UUA developed workshops designed to reduce prejudice by increasing understanding and acceptance among people of different sexual orientations. Bishop brought this initiative to the attention of the committee, and Polly Talen and Wagner began working on the process of certifying First Universalist as a Welcoming Congregation. On May 13, 1993, the church was among the first to be certified by the UUA.

At the suggestion of Sweetser, the church began holding 4x4 dinners in 1992, mixing GLBT and straight people. Over the next year, church members learned about gay issues and participated in the Twin Cities GLBT Pride Festival.

An AIDS quilt hand-made by members and friends of the church was combined with hundreds of other such quilts on the turf of the Metrodome stadium in Minneapolis, circa 1992.

In 1996, the United States Congress narrowly rejected a bill to ban discrimination in the workplace against gays and lesbians, and overwhelmingly passed the Defense of Marriage Act, which barred states from sanctioning same-sex marriages. In response, the Reverends Sheryl Wurl and Ken Brown, First Universalist's interim ministers, asked the board to declare the church a hate-free zone, which it did. On October 13, 1996, the congregation marched around the building in a symbolic declaration, singing "Circle Round for Freedom." The event got television media coverage.

From a gay parenting group that met at First Universalist, the organization Rainbow Families was formed in June 1997. A year later the church hosted Rainbow Families' annual banquet. An active Interweave chapter started at the church in 1998, led by A.J. Galazen, who led the first Pride service. In 2001, Interweave sent a proposal to the board to increase training and education about bisexuality and transgender issues, as transsexual and transgender individuals were welcomed into First Universalist Church.

In March 2004, opponents of gay marriage organized an effort to amend the state constitution forbidding it. As a result of a conversation on the Cyber Coffeehour the congregation mobilized, and at a special meeting on April 4, 2004, approved a resolution. A few days later members turned out in record numbers for Lobby Day at the state Capitol to oppose the amendment.

In 2006, sabbatical support minister, the Reverend Ted Tollefson, challenged the congregation to turn out more people at the Capitol for a rally against the proposed amendment than friends from St. Paul's Unity Church-Unitarian would. More than 100 First Universalists showed up on a weekday to demonstrate solidarity with the GLBT community, and Tollefson won his bet with the Reverend Rob Eller-Isaacs of Unity Church-Unitarian.

—*Jessica Wicks, including notes provided by John Addington*

From Unity House to the First Universalist Foundation

The Church of the Redeemer was the primary sponsor of Unity House when it was formed in 1897. The church established a separate non-profit corporation called The Unity Settlement Association for this purpose. When the settlement house was condemned in 1968 to make way for freeway development, the condemnation proceeds were placed into a trust called The Unity Settlement Association Trust, with First Universalist Church as the trustee.

Unity House cooking class

The Unity Settlement Association continued in existence, but instead of operating a settlement house and related programs, it made grants from the money received from the trust. The Unity Settlement Association was also the beneficiary of the Stephenson and Boutell funds administered through the Minneapolis Foundation.

In 1983, the Unity Settlement Association was dissolved and the grant-making function was transferred directly to First Universalist Church to avoid potential tax problems. The trust agreement had a provision that stated what was to happen if the Unity Settlement Association ceased to exist. Article V (a) of the trust agreement provided as follows: *If Unity should ever cease to exist, The Trust shall terminate and any accumulated income and trust principal shall become the property of Church which shall then determine an appropriate use or disposition of the assets; provided, however, that such disposition shall be limited to purposes of social concern and that none of the assets shall be used for the general operating purposes or capital improvements of Church or become a part of the general assets of Church.*

Unity Summer (below) is a major beneficiary of the First Universalist Foundation, which started from our original beneficiary, Unity House.

At the 1983 Annual Meeting, the members of First Universalist adopted a resolution to accept the funds from the trust "consistent with the restrictions in the Trust Agreement." The church formed a committee to develop a plan for administering the funds and created the structure for the First Universalist Foundation. At the 1984 annual meeting, the

First Universalist Foundation acts as a catalyst for social change by promoting and supporting the development of emerging leaders among youth, young adults, and disenfranchised communities through monetary grants to and partnerships with non-profits working in those communities.

— The First Universalist Foundation Mission Statement, revised April 2008

For many years, the Foundation provided about half of Unity Summer's budget, with annual funding of $8,000.

In 2008, the Foundation provided a grant of $22,000 to pay youth stipends in the program.

In 2009, the Foundation funded the $45,000 needed for stipends to be paid to 30 youth from around the Twin Cities and for the program's summer mentors.

Foundation, with its own board, was created.

In the early days of the Foundation, the board funded a number of local nonprofit agencies with small grants. A long-standing controversy was whether it was appropriate to use Foundation money for the salary of the church's Social Justice Coordinator. The concern was that this was a staff position and Foundation funds were not to be used for the operation of the church. On the other hand it was clear that the Social Justice Coordinator advanced the social justice agenda of the church, an agenda that was clearly within the guidelines of the Unity Settlement Association.

The 2008-2009 church year was a time of transition for the Foundation. Writing in the annual report, Foundation board chair Eric Cooperstein said: " In recent years, the Foundation has made a series of small grants ranging from $1,000 to $5,000 (totaling about $40,000) and a single larger grant of about $20,000. As part of our refocused mission and values, the foundation is transitioning to making fewer but larger grants. At the same time, we have renewed and deepened our commitment to the Unity Leadership Institute (formerly Unity Summer)."

The Foundation report had this to say about the $45,000 grant to Unity Leadership Institute in 2009: "Although this grant consumed most of Foundation's funds this year, we are unanimous in our support for this unique, transformative program that is tied so closely to the values of Unitarian Universalism. Nearly every member of the Foundation board volunteered in some capacity at one of the two Unity Leadership retreats held this spring. The Foundation is committed to the development of this remarkable program."

The Foundation's capacity for giving grew impressively. The fund balance on June 30, 1982, was $238,000. In spite of the severe economic downturn in 2008 and 2009, the fund balance was roughly $1 million at the time of the congregation's annual meeting in 2009. The success of the First Universalist Foundation is yet another example of the vision, stewardship, and commitment to justice that has characterized the First Universalist Church.

—information from Gene Link

FROM UNITY SUMMER TO UNITY LEADERSHIP INSTITUTE: YOUNG PEOPLE MAKING THEIR MARK

We care enough to do something about it. We care enough to put some of our resources as a community behind it. We care enough to put you on the line, and to be there with you, to take it in the face with you. That's why Bob Knuth, our social justice and youth coordinator, along with you and some adults in our community, have proposed we launch an urban action job corps for our kids and kids in our new community. We will team kids with adult mentors and place them in social service agencies. . . . Our plan includes places in equal number for neighborhood kids. We can make that sacred village work now.
— the Reverend Terry Sweetser's sermon, "In Your Face," March 7, 1993, announcing Unity Summer

Unity Leadership Institute, 2008

Around the time of the move to the Dupont church building in 1993, the Reverend Terry Sweetser envisioned a major social justice initiative that would engage youth and adults in a ministry to the Minneapolis community. He and Bob Knuth, First Universalist's social justice coordinator and youth advisor, worked with a group of volunteers to launch the Unity Summer program in 1993 with a grant from the Veatch Foundation of the Unitarian Universalist Congregation at Shelter Rock in Long Island, New York.

Unity Summer took its name from and built on the heritage of Unity House established in 1897. According to Unity House's first annual report, they had "no creed but the golden rule and work for man." Unity House provided a safe environment where people were mentored and empowered to develop skills they would carry with them for the rest of their lives. Unity Summer was also envisioned as an outreach program, with the goal of creating a new generation of change agents.

A group of youth and adults from First Universalist Church worked with Sweetser and Knuth in 1993 to examine how to creatively address the needs of Minneapolis' young people and the larger community. They committed to developing a program that would employ youth from a variety of backgrounds in environments that would encourage them to consider careers in the non-profit sector while simultaneously providing volunteer assistance to social welfare organizations operating with minimal

Quotes from Unity Summer interns

"Problems exist because we let them exist. If we were to stand up to it, the problem wouldn't exist."
—Kia Her

"Community is more than the people we live next to."
—Dylan Leavitt-Phibbs

"Without communities in the world nothing can change, because the power of many outshines the power of one."
—Mikesha Barnes

The Unity Summer Circle was given to First Universalist by Welcome Jerde and Dan Berg in 2007, in memory and honor of their daughter, Julia, a Unity Summer intern.

Betsy Allis was the program chair of Unity Summer in the 1990s, succeeded by Marcia Wattson, Jennifer Schuster-Jaeger, and Judy Broad. Jean Buckley volunteered for Unity Summer every year since its inception. In 2004, social justice coordinator Debra Rodgers managed the expansion of the leadership program. Summer coordinators have included Quiana Perkins and Carol Martignacco. Several former interns have been hired to serve as mentors.

financial resources. That summer 38 young people from the church and the surrounding community were hired and placed in 16 social justice agencies. The interns were paid $4.50 per hour for 20 hours of work per week for 8 weeks. The interns had regular meetings with a paid Unity Summer coordinator and church members who volunteered as mentors. They attended weekly seminars, were supervised at their work site, and made a public presentation of their experiences. The original budget was $35,000.

At the Unity Summer banquet at the end of the program, interns present what they have learned. Many of the presentations have been quite moving, as interns shared experiences of working with mothers and children at the Harriet Tubman women's shelter or getting to know the clients at Simpson Transitional Housing or The Aliveness Project.

In 2004, the program shifted from providing service to a more explicit emphasis on creating social change. Workshops for participants focused on the skills needed for change: how to build intentional relationships; the role of community; oppression and racial justice; understanding power; and developing critical thinking tools to get to the root causes of problems. Young adult mentors facilitated the workshops and provided a safe experience for youth to reflect on what they learned.

In 2006, the Unity Leadership retreat was added to provide an intensive weekend experience that focused on identity, values, decision making and living in a multi-cultural world. The retreats stood on their own as powerful learning tools for youth and also served as the live action interview for admission into the Unity Summer Internship program. As many as 35 agencies have partnered with the program, including helping to develop and manage the program. The First Universalist Foundation has expanded its financial support and by 2009 considered Unity Summer the Foundation's primary recipient of funding.

The mission of Unity Summer, now Unity Leadership Institute, is to connect, engage and empower youth to work for social change. This program has developed as a way for the church to honor the gifts of its founders—gifts of ideas, liberty, religious values and justice.

—*Debra Rodgers and Judy Broad, with information from Marcia Wattson*

One Unity Leadership Experience

I would never have had the confidence and opportunity to be speaking to you [at the Unity Summer banquet] if I didn't get accepted into The Unity Summer Leadership program. I was one of 25 students from across the Twin Cities chosen to experience what different social justice organizations do for our community. The hardest part of this experience was the workshops that taught me to open up to peers that are different from me in appearance and lifestyle. It took a lot of courage for [us] . . . to let down our defenses and talk openly about ourselves and examine our views. I learned to be proud of my identity and values but also to respect the values and identity of others. Most of all I learned that youth of all races and cultures have a voice . . . We will face our fears bravely, and empower a new generation of youth working for social change. — *Tianna Reyes, Unity Leadership Intern, 2008*

Unity Summer: Two Profiles

Aaron and Beth Stelson, who grew up at First Universalist, participated in the Unity Summer Program as high school students. Both attest to the powerful effect the program had on their world views and choice of careers.

Aaron was an intern at Horizons Youth Center in 1998 and continued as Unity Summer's youth co-chair during the summers of 1999-2001. He graduated from Brown University with a focus on urban studies and civil engineering, and went on to MIT for a masters in urban planning. After finishing a two-year commitment with Teach for America, Aaron designed a service learning program designed after Unity Summer for a high school in New Haven, Connecticut, in fall 2009. As Aaron explained: *Unity Summer gave me my first real exposure to people who lived a life very different from my own in terms of race and socio-economic status. Though I didn't realize it then, working with low-income youth at Horizons Youth Center started me on a path toward a life of service, realizing the privileges and accompanying responsibilities I had. Though participating in the program was valuable, I think serving as the youth co-chair of Unity Summer had a larger impact on my life. From that position, I went on to lead service-learning projects in college and continue to lead service-learning projects for high school students.*

Beth joined Unity Summer in 2002 as an intern at Walker Methodist Health Center. After graduating from Brown University in 2008 with a focus on women's history and gender issues, Beth completed an internship with the Aliveness Project, a community center for those diagnosed with AIDS, before joining an environmental outreach project in New Orleans. As she explained: *Working at Walker Methodist Health Center provided an intimate understanding of the importance of compassion, common ground, and intergenerational connection. However, the lasting impact was the exposure to the diversity of non-profit organizations that participated in Unity Summer. Learning about the existence of these non-profits and listening to my fellow Unity Summer participants elaborate on common issues they encountered taught me the necessity of cooperation among social justice organizations. The need to increase inter-agency cooperation and to pool non-profit resources will now bring me to New Orleans where I will connect local non-profits to help low-income families rebuild their homes at a rebuilding organization called The Green Project.*

WORKING FOR PEACE SINCE WORLD WAR II

Unity House (1897-1968) was a profound example of early Universalist commitment to community support for the new and less fortunate. This article picks up that thread and adds examples of national and international human rights efforts of the congregation during the last half of the twentieth century.

As the shrunken First Universalist congregation of 40 emerged from World War II, members committed themselves to the bold step of building a new church during the ministry of the Reverend Carl Olson. Many members organized to welcome international students into their homes who were studying for degrees at the University of Minnesota and other Twin Cities colleges, a program that lasted about 15 years.

Tom Atchison, pictured at the World Citizen table, was a long-time chair of the Pathways to Peace project, which brought attention to non-violence in world affairs and promoted actions for peace.

Civil Rights and the Vietnam War

When civil rights issues broke out in the early 1960s, the Reverend John Cummins joined hundreds of other ministers and citizens in protesting police brutality against black Americans in Selma, Alabama, in 1965. Widespread demonstrations in other cities led to the passage by the United States Congress of the landmark Civil Rights Act of 1964 and the Voting Rights Act in 1965.

When the Vietnam War incited growing public opposition and demonstrations, Cummins provided leadership from both the pulpit and the street. Not only did he inveigh against war as a solution, he counseled dozens of youth regarding conscientious objector status. In one case, he provided temporary sanctuary to a demonstrator being threatened by police at an anti-war parade near the church.

Racial justice issues moved back into the forefront a generation later, under the ministerial leadership of the Reverends Terry Sweetser and Susan Milnor. Several initiatives were tried, the first one taking the form of a joint venture with 10 black churches on Minneapolis' north side to share culture and explore joint forms of worship. First Universalist gained an appreciation for gospel music with a choir exchange, as well as the deep-rooted sense of faith in God and the Bible. When no sustainable form of common worship could be established, the effort was disbanded. Internally, however, well-attended workshops were held on white privilege and diversity training.

Central American Human Rights
With reports of mass atrocities against citizens and church leaders such as Archbishop Oscar Romero in El Salvador in 1980, Central American terrorism became a flash point for congregational action. U.S. tax dollars were being spent by the Reagan administration to support totalitarian regimes there, driving Central Americans to seek sanctuary in U.S. churches. First Universalist responded in 1984, voting 130-7 to declare itself a sanctuary church. It was the 90th of 120 U.S. churches to open their doors to such terror victims, and the third of three Minneapolis area churches to commit this act of civil disobedience.

The church first housed a Guatemalan couple (who declined to speak out publicly) and then Marlon Machado, a young Salvadoran. Machado's arrival was covered in an article in the *Minneapolis Star Tribune* on February 1, 1985, announcing that First Universalist Church would host a meeting of the Twin Cities Sanctuary movement.

Under the leadership of Dick and Marie Saunders, more than 150 church members and individuals from the community maintained around-the-clock protection, prepared meals, and arranged speaking engagements, social visits with countrymen and women, and consultation services with a priest. Congregants traveled to national meetings to coordinate strategies with other sanctuary churches, meeting Rigoberto Menchu, Nobel Peace Prize-winning Guatemalan activist, at one. After Machado left in 1985 to join friends in southern California,

In the course of the war in Vietnam I counseled young draft resisters . . . well over 500 young men somehow found their way to the church to have counseling. . . . There was George Crocker. George told me -- he was a very tall, lanky young man -- that he had participated in a protest at the University wearing an Uncle Sam uniform and carrying a sandwich board on which was written, "Stop the Draft" or something similar, and the FBI had spotted him. So he and his girlfriend hopped in his car and drove over to the church. I told him they could, indeed, stay. . . . George and his girlfriend sat themselves on the altar steps. Eventually half a dozen sympathizers appeared and there they all sat. . . . The FBI pulled up across the street and called me, asking me to send George and his friends out, and I said that I would not do that. . . . [Eventually] they came in and took George away. I don't know how long he was in prison, but that is the kind of thing that would happen.
—the Reverend John Cummins, in an interview with church members, 1981

the Sanctuary committee evolved into a Latin American Affairs committee. That committee wrote protest letters to Minnesota congressional members, hosted human rights speakers from Central American citizen groups fighting terrorism, and opposed the U.S.-funded Contra war.

Pioneering Environmental Programs

The congregation's interest in addressing environmental threats came after Rachel Carson's book *Silent Spring* was published in 1962, documenting DDT's dangers to plant and bird life. Action burst forth with the national celebration of Earth Day on April 1, 1970, and the subsequent formation of a church Environmental Action Committee. The committee sponsored educational forums with guest speakers from all phases of the budding environmental movement, including solar energy and sustainable agriculture, and undertook energy-saving measures to reduce reliance on foreign oil. President Carter asked the nation to turn down the thermostat and wear a sweater. We did.

U.S. Senator Paul Wellstone with the Reverends Terry Sweetser and Susan Milnor (below), after the Minnesota Senator spoke about social justice at First Universalist in 1991.

The Environmental Action Committee raised awareness with study groups on simple living, responsible consumption, sustainable agriculture, biodiversity, toxic chemicals, buying locally grown food from community suppliers, and other promotions to encourage green behaviors. The committee launched a holiday gift exchange in 2000, which became one of the church's most popular annual traditions. It also worked closely with the Building and Grounds Committee to conduct periodic energy audits and execute recommended changes, resulting in significant energy and monetary savings.

The committee took on a new life in 2004, after the Economic Globalization group changed its name to EcoMinds and its focus to global warming, giving rise to a global warming theme for the 2004 Earth Day celebration. EcoMinds became an official MUUSJA working group in 2005, leaving First Universalist's EcoMinds to focus both on sustainable practices and Earth Day, with the larger legislative advocacy and education work of MUUSJA being done in partnership with

Congregations Caring for Creation. In 2008 EcoMinds proposed that the church become a certified UU Green Sanctuary.

Evolution of our Social Action Strategy and Direction
In 1990 the report of a Social Action Task Force, convened by Sharon Bishop, described the Social Justice program: "Despite our strengths, there is dissatisfaction with the organization and scope of our social action program. . . . Those most actively involved want greater coordination and communication." Subsequently, 100 congregants met at a retreat to review the church's commitment, activities and structure related to social action. A five-year plan was created with a focus on three projects—an Early Childhood Learning Center partnership, Adequate Housing, and Environmental Concerns—as well as providing for a paid professional social action coordinator.

Minnesota UU Social Justice Alliance (MUUSJA)

In 2001, council director Betsy Allis (right) and Social Justice coordinator Jo Haberman joined with former member and Social Justice Council director Lois Hamilton and Unitarian Universalist (UU) minister the Reverend Wendy Jerome to propose the founding of the area's first UU multi-issue congregation-based community organizing group: the Metro UU Social Justice Alliance. MUUSJA's founding meeting was held with 35 UUs in attendance from eight churches.

Within a month of that meeting, the attacks of September 11th occurred, inspiring MUUSJA to respond with its first program. A December forum at First Universalist, "Understanding Terrorism: Developing Strategies for Peace After September 11," attended by more than 250 UUs from 11 congregations. A follow-up planning meeting was held with 100 participants, who voted to focus efforts on working groups that would explore economic globalization and Mideast peace. Other groups were formed in later years. First Universalist members played key roles in starting and leading each of the working groups. MUUSJA's name changed to Minnesota UU Social Justice Alliance after a statewide UU organizing campaign on marriage equality, co-led by Ralph Wyman.

MUUSJA's mission is to bring together UUs to work collectively for social change by building a lasting social change organization; preparing UUs to use the standard organizing technique of reflection, action, and collaboration; developing a distinctly UU moral voice; and waging campaigns in coalition with interfaith and secular partners.

Tom Esch, pictured above right with eventual United States Congressman Keith Ellison, was hired as Social Justice Coordinator. Esch had a gift for engaging new people and helping activists ground their work in UU values. When Esch left in 2000, he was replaced by long-time community organizer Jo Haberman.

Ministerial student Sheryl Wurl worked part time to help launch the three central projects and fund a full-time coordinator. The Veatch Foundation of the Congregation of Shelter Rock in New York awarded $40,000 to fund the position and projects, making it possible for Bob Knuth to become the first full-time social justice coordinator in the Unitarian Universalist denomination. Veatch added another $10,000 in 1994 in recognition of the Unity Summer program.

Movement Toward Advocacy

Knuth resigned in 1994, leaving community minister, the Reverend Gretchen Thompson, to carve out hours to work with Nancy Atchison and other members to identify priorities for the next five years. The Social Justice Council, which coordinated the congregation's social justice activities, began differentiating the church's justice work in terms of education and advocacy (six groups) and hands-on service (seven groups).

In 1995, the Social Justice Council sponsored a workshop on the arts of democracy as an organizing strategy, with writer activists Frances Moore Lappe and Paul Martin Dubois. More than 100 church members attended. Although the energy generated by their ideas was palpable, momentum was lost during the transition that ensued when Sweetser and Milnor left in 1995.

Another renewal period started in 2000 when a newly formed Social Justice Council steering committee, chaired by Betsy Allis and staffed by Social Justice Coordinator Jo Haberman, launched an effort to engage the congregation in creating and achieving a shared vision of justice. This was done with visioning dialogues, interactive kiosks, study circles on Richard Gilbert's book, *The Prophetic Imperative,* and a daylong social justice retreat held at Our Lady of Lourdes Catholic Church. Out of this renewal work came the development of the church's first Model of Social Justice that included guiding principles and tools for approaching the work.

— *Dick Saunders and Betsy Allis*

Snapshot of Deeds and Interests

1995: First Universalist members organized The Pro-Choice Cookie Brigade. Members baked cookies that were brought to abortion clinics. Cards delivered with the cookies read, "First Universalist Church of Minneapolis sends you support, admiration and cookies to enjoy and share. Thanks for providing women with a choice!"

1996: A survey of First Universalist members revealed that the leading social justice activities were Welcoming Congregation (71), Habitat for Humanity (55), Loaves and Fishes (49), Interweave (25), environmental issues (18).

2004: A special meeting of the congregation was held to consider two resolutions. 1) Do you support the proposed resolution to support every person's right to reproductive choice and endorse the Association of Universalist Women's co-sponsorship of the March for Women's Lives, to be held in Washington, D.C., on April 25, 2004? 2) Do you support the proposed resolution to oppose any constitutional amendment to ban the legal recognition of same-sex marriages, civil unions, and/or domestic-partner registries? The vote was 165 to 0 in support of the first, and 165 to 1 on the second.

2005: The First Universalist Foundation approved grants for organizations that developed African immigrant training videos, anti-bias curriculum materials and training programs, computer technology training for Spanish-speaking adults, engagement of parents and Minneapolis school board members in Somali literacy programs, and a performance and support opportunity for gay, lesbian, bisexual and transgendered youth.

2007: Unity Summer interns were involved with the Tubman Family Alliance's National Night Out teen health awareness and Peace Camp; Sierra Club's Cool Cities community events; MICAH's door knocking to gain support for affordable housing and increased transportation.

—*information from notes kept by John Addington*

Human rights activist, Nobel Peace Prize recipient and Holocaust survivor Elie Wiesel, holding hands with his wife, visits the First Universalist peace pole with Sharon Bishop and Tom Atchison

The gifts that we have received from those who have come before us—this church, Lakewood, the ideas of religious liberty, our spiritual community—have sustained us in times of trouble and helped us find the courage to meet the challenges of life, liberty, and the pursuit of happiness.
— First Universalist member and Minnesota Secretary of State Mark Ritchie

WORLD CITIZEN LYNN ELLING

When we think of First Universalist Church, we think of people —wonderful people who were and are out in the world doing. People like Lynn Elling, who raised everyone's consciousness on world citizenship long before global education became popular. We remember traveling in Europe with our children in 1972 on a World Citizen passport Lynn arranged for us. We had mixed reception at the various borders . . . [some] guards read the passport, looked at our picture, smiled, and talked about the wonderful concept of world citizenship.
— *Don and Helen Ryberg, 1992*

Lynn Elling (left) presented a plaque to board president David Lauth during the installation of First Universalist's Peace Pole, which is a handcrafted monument that displays the message "May Peace Prevail on Earth." Each side of the pole displays the message in four to 16 languages reflecting the community's population. More than 200,000 Peace Poles have been planted in 180 countries throughout the world.

As a World War II Naval Officer Lynn Elling saw the carnage of the battle of Tarawa where 6,000 people were killed. From this point on he was haunted by the question, "How can we abolish war?" In 1954 Lynn and his wife, Donna, traveled to Hiroshima, Japan, where his life was changed and he made a commitment to do whatever he could to promote a just and peaceful world. His passion led to an amazing accomplishment in 1971, when all of Minnesota's major political and civic leaders signed a Declaration of World Citizenship (originally housed at 5000 Girard Avenue South).

Elling, the father of five, directed much of his effort toward working in schools. In 1982 he founded World Citizen, Inc., and introduced the Peace Site Program. There are more than 750 peace sites worldwide, with more than 200 in Minnesota. First Universalist was designated as one of the world's first peace sites in 1988.

Elling was the co-founder of the Nobel Peace Prize Festival held each year at Augsburg College in Minneapolis. Elling, whose roots as a Universalist began in the Church of the Redeemer Sunday School in 1923, remained active at First Universalist Church in 2009, along with his wife.

The founding of World Citizen Inc., on United Nations Sunday, October 23, 1982, featured (left to right): Lynn Elling, Dr. Richard Green, Jack Edie, and the Reverend John Cummins

ILLUMINATE THE PAST, CELEBRATE THE PRESENT, INSPIRE THE FUTURE

*Each of us, a pilgrim,
climbs eternally the mountain of
the past,
and when we reach the peak,
and see what is to be seen
therefrom,
we lie down upon that mountain
of human experience,
and the small measure of our
dust adds to its height,
whereby our peers, companions,
and those who come after us
may see a small way
further than we.*

—the Reverend John Cummins

Bearing Witness and Looking Ahead

Maypole dancers at the intergenerational service and picnic at Lake Harriet Bandshell in Minneapolis, celebrating First Universalist's 150 years

On October 24, 2009, First Universalist Church of Minneapolis was 150 years old, a venerable age for any institution. It was a time to reflect, to honor the legacy of those who came before, yes, but not a time to rest on past history, not a time to slumber. The congregation embraced the sesquicentennial with gusto and with a spirit of gratitude, humility, and celebration. The congregation is proud of its history and embraced it as an inspiration for renewal and as a challenge for the future. The task was to honor the ancestors by knowing the history and building on that cherished legacy.

This brief section, *Illuminate the Past, Celebrate the Present, Inspire the Future*, takes its name from the 150th anniversary logo. We pause here to note the anniversary commemorations at 50 and 100 years, significant moments in our history when we reflected on our heritage and dreamed of our future. We linger a bit longer at the 150 year mark, the sesquicentennial celebration that led to the creation and publication of this book.

It is significant that the anniversary coincided with the calling of a new young minister, Justin Schroeder, a man raised in Unitarian Universalist churches who came with a powerful vision not only of hope for the future, but of responsibility. "I believe it is my responsibility," he wrote, "to bear witness to the Universal Love and underlying unity that holds us all, and that invites us to become fully human, alive, and of service to something larger than ourselves. I have dedicated my life to this vision."

This section closes with words from Schroeder as he joins with the congregation to inspire the future of the First Universalist Church of Minnesota.

Illuminate the Past
The First 50 Years

At the first commemoration of First Universalist's history—the celebration of the Reverend James Tuttle's 25 years as our settled minister in 1891—Boston's Universalist Publishing House published a 362-page book, *The Field and The Fruit: A Memorial of Twenty-Five Years' Ministry with the Church of the Redeemer, Minneapolis*. Tuttle "affectionately dedicated" the book to the congregation. It is a beautiful collection of Tuttle's thoughts and recollections, 12 of his favorite sermons, and a tribute from the Reverend Marion Shutter, then his assistant minister of five years. Much of the book, including the sermons, is about sowing the seeds of the future. In "Down Growing and Upward Fruiting," Tuttle said:

The Reverend James Tuttle, seated center with a garden party, was a beloved and progressive minister who led the church for 25 years.

Our root-life, life below ground, is that part of us which draws its sustenance from the past; while our upper life, life above ground, stalk-life, is related more to the present and future. As the tree cannot stand erect and bear fruit, except it have support from beneath, so we cannot attain our best position and reach the highest results without extracting life and power from things behind us. . . . Every people, every literature, and every religion has a history to feed its life on to some extent. But our life is not altogether a product of the past; and it should not rely wholly, nor chiefly, on the past. Rising above its hidden roots, a tree draws sustenance also from the air and the light, from the summer dew and rain.

We should be, but are not always, both conservative and progressive. We should stand firm on something, be fixed in something, and at the same time reach up and forward for something. . . . One who cuts loose from history . . . to whom the word 'conservative' has become obsolete or a mark for ridicule is like a tree trying to stand upright to enlarge its branches and make a fair show among its fellows, after letting go of the ground. Our present age has been particularly an age of discovery, of invention, of new things, and hence there has been born out of it a spirit of impatience toward the past and a blind longing for novelty. . . . The error of making such a chase for new things as to leave the old out of sight is of course not greater than the error of being so wedded to the old, so encased in it, so prejudiced by it, as to cause one to refuse any further investigation or instruction.

This cup was presented to William D. Washburn at the 50th anniversary celebration. A Washburn descendant donated it to First Universalist, where it is now housed.

There could be, of course, volumes written of the work done by our church; but who can estimate the unseen or spiritual help? The pioneer work was not all done in the [eighteen]sixties. There is plenty to spare and here and now!

—Mrs. Louise Morgan Lovejoy, 1909, at the 50th anniversary celebration of Church of the Redeemer

Eighteen years later, in 1909, the Church of the Redeemer gathered together for two days of celebrations in honor of its 50th anniversary. There were sermons, hymns, and an elaborate banquet. A 63-page booklet lovingly preserved the many tributes and addresses of the weekend, including those of long-time members William D. Washburn, Major William D. Hale, Charles M. Loring, and William P. Roberts. The closing address was given by Judge Martin B. Koon, who said: *"As we glance for a moment at the history of this Church, four names stand out more prominently than all others—James H. Tuttle, Marion D. Shutter, William D. Washburn and Dorilus Morrison. . . . Of Dr. Tuttle's character and work in this community . . . his boundless charity, his great love, his all-embracing sympathy, his tender heart, reached out and touched every phase of human sorrow, suffering and sin wherever found, and there was always healing, help and consolation in the touch. Is it any wonder, therefore, that Dr. Tuttle's influence for good in this city was greater than that of any other man, and that he was most universally loved and respected, and that his name is now so reverently cherished by the people to whom he ministered so long and loved so well?"*

Of Shutter, then in the 18th year of his pastorate, Koon said: *"He has developed into practical use the idea that the true mission of a minister of the gospel is not alone to prepare humanity for the life hereafter—of which we know so little—but as well to help them to live better, purer, nobler lives in this world—of which we know so much—to give people cleaner streets in which to walk, purer air to breathe, better homes, more wholesome surroundings, and in every way to improve their moral, physical and social condition here on earth."*

Koon would not know that in the first 120 years of First Universalist Church, the church would have only four remarkably long-standing ministers. But he did know that in its first 50 years, the church had only two presidents of its Board of Trustees. As he said, *"Mr. Morrison and Mr. Washburn came to Minneapolis from the same state, impelled by the same ambitions, buoyed by the same hopes and inspired by the same religious convictions. Shoulder to shoulder, hand in hand, they worked together faithfully and unselfishly to build up and sustain the Church of the Redeemer. They were its two strongest bulwarks and supporters during all of its trying history."*

Morrison had died 12 years earlier. Koons presented Washburn with an inscribed silver cup for his years of service, saying: "While it may appear to you to be empty, it is in fact filled to overflowing with the sincerest respect, the deepest gratitude and tenderest love of this Church and all its people for you."

ILLUMINATE THE PAST
100 YEARS

When First Universalist Church of Minneapolis gathered in 1959 to commemorate the 100 year anniversary, the speakers inspired the celebrants with their forward-thinking vision.

The church had survived the lean years of wartime. The Reverend Carl Olson had led the congregation to a new location at 5000 Girard and the church was growing again. The Reverend Sophia Fahs, a Unitarian minister and curriculum consultant for the Council of Liberal Churches, gave the keynote speech at an elegant dinner at the Curtis Hotel in Minneapolis. Fahs spoke on "The Church in a Children's Century." She was a revolutionary thinker on the liberal religious education of children. When she first taught Sunday school at the turn of the century, the Bible was represented as doctrine. She warned then that children would grow up to walk away from religion if the approach to educating them was not changed. In a *UUWorld* article about her in 2003, she was quoted as saying, "To build the beginnings of faith in God on a conception of the universe that our generation no longer regards as true is to prepare the way for a loss of respect for the Bible; and what is worse, to court a cynical atheism when the child is old enough to learn for himself."

The Reverend Sophia Fahs, pictured with the Reverend Carl Olson, was ordained at age 83 shortly before she gave the keynote address in celebration of First Universalist's 100th anniversary.

First Universalist Church congregants gathered at the Curtis Hotel on October 24, 1959, to celebrate 100 years of history with a dinner of roast turkey and pumpkin pie, and a benediction by the Reverend Philip Giles, general superintendent of the Universalist Church of America.

Lynn Elling, at the podium, presided over the 100th anniversary celebration as board president and 50 years later, attended the 150th anniversary celebration.

As Unitarian—and Universalist—membership shrank nationwide, Fahs' ideas began to be taken more seriously. One of her many books, *The Church Across the Street* (1947), is the basis for Unitarian Universalist Association's *Neighboring Faiths* curriculum.

In the 100-year anniversary sermon, First Universalist Church assistant minister and religious education director the Reverend Kenneth Marshall described the church's pioneering heritage and outlined the work that needed to be done in the coming decades. His list of challenges for First Universalist Church and the wider world included:

- Becoming technologically one world, breaking down physical barriers;
- Tearing down barriers: "Religious exclusivism—Christian, Jewish, Muslim—can contribute to the destruction of the human race";
- Continuing reform in mental hygiene, public health, education;
- Destroying artificial barriers such as class or race discrimination;
- Establishing world law;
- Ongoing pioneering work in religious education.

Marshall suggested working in tandem with the Quakers, with ethical societies, and with the liberal wings of other denominations to accomplish all that needed to be done to build a better world. Marshall also pointed out that forms of authoritarianism were well organized—the Catholic church, Billy Graham, Communism—and said that religious liberals had missed key opportunities to effect change because of an historic reluctance to organize and to proclaim beliefs. There might be millions of people in America who, he said, "are inclined our way, if they only knew about us . . . We stand on the threshold of the nuclear and space age, with its revolutionary changes and implications. Again the climate of thought in America is favorable for an advance in liberal religion. We dare not muff this chance.

"What will the world be like a century hence—in 2059? . . . Will the earth be the home of free men, prosperous and orderly under some form of liberal world law . . . having solved many of today's problems?"
—*Mikki Morrissette*

CELEBRATE THE PRESENT
150 YEARS

The Church celebrated other significant anniversaries—the 90th, 125th, 135th—but it was the 150th that captured the imagination of so many and that presented the opportunity to probe the legacy of our past more deeply, to reflect on the deeds and spirit of the present, and to plan and dream for the future. The 150th motif, *Illuminate the Past, Celebrate the Present, Inspire the Future* was a true touchstone for a year-long examination of the First Universalist Church of Minneapolis. It was a journey that was surprising at times, sometimes deeply moving, always informative. This book is one culmination of that journey, a tangible reminder of the care and persistence of the many people who loved First Universalist Church and cherished its history.

The sesquicentennial celebration was launched October 25 and 26, 2008, a year before the actual anniversary. The weekend began with 130 First Universalists gathering on Saturday to hear presentations by three noted Unitarian Universalist theologians, ministers, and historians. The Reverend Paul Rasor, Unitarian Universalist (UU) minister, theologian and the director of the Center for the Study of Religious Freedom at Virginia Wesleyan College opened with "Circumscribing Universalism: Navigating Some Universalist Shoals." He quoted the Reverend Robert Cummins, father of Minister Emeritus John Cummins and former head of the Universalist Church of America, as saying "a circumscribed Universalism is unthinkable."

The Reverend Dr. Elizabeth Strong, a student of Universalist history and a UU minister of religious education, spoke on "Universalism's Long and Proud History: its people, theologies, scholarship and just plain quirkiness." She was followed by John Hurley, the Unitarian Universalist Association archivist and director of communications, who read articles about the congregation's 50th and 100th anniversaries from the *Universalist/Christian Leader*, a predecessor to *UUWorld* magazine. Hurley emphasized the importance of history in answering the questions of what people need to be reconciled to and what wounds need to be healed. On Sunday, Rasor preached on "Democracy Matters," and Strong shared excerpts from the Reverend Marion Shutter's 10-sermon series about evolution, which he preached at the turn of the twentieth century to crowds of more than a thousand.

It is worth recalling that one of the core themes of early Universalism was hope . . . the liberating vision at the core of our faith tradition is a basis for hope today. It is the vision we must keep before us as we go forward, the picture we must keep in mind as we circumscribe a revitalized Unitarian Universalism for our time. In doing this, we are honoring Robert Cummins' call to make it "unmistakably clear that all are welcome: theist and humanist, unitarian and trinitarian, colored, and color-less."
—the Reverend Paul Rasor, October 25, 2008, at the Sesquicentennial Kick-off Weekend for the First Universalist Church of Minneapolis

The Sesquicentennial Soiree

The Sesquicentennial Soiree, held April 18, 2009, was the party we'd been waiting for. The Reverend Kate Tucker's vision of "all of us there" was realized with over 430 people in attendance. At Tucker's suggestion, there were two empty chairs at the Soiree: "one to honor those church members who have gone before, on whose shoulders we stand, and one for those we may never see, the ones for whom we labor, the ones who'll seek and find us in the next decade and the next and the next."

150th anniversary keynote speaker the Reverend Lee Barker, president of Meadville-Lombard Theological School, was raised and ordained at First Universalist.

After a lively social hour with music director John Jensen tinkling the keys of his clavichord, the program began with a welcome from Karin Wille, co-chair of the Sesquicentennial Steering Committee. Following an elegant dinner, Nancy Atchison, Steering Committee co-chair, introduced First Universalist Minister Emeritus, the Reverend John Cummins, who described his long relationship with the keynote speaker, the Reverend Dr. Lee Barker. Cummins ministered to Barker as a young man and conscientious objector during the Vietnam War. Barker filled in more of the story in his presentation, "The Last Living Universalist Tells All," in which he pointed out that universal salvation is relevant even today.

Noted folk singer Ann Reed closed with several ballads and led the gathering in singing "We Will," the sesquicentennial song that she was commissioned to compose for the church.

INSPIRE THE FUTURE
150 YEARS OF THINKING AHEAD

Our church should help to shape the future, not merely react to it.
—Mission statement of the First Universalist Church Futures Committee, 1979

When the First Universalist Church of Minneapolis formed a Futures Committee in 1979, the intention was to identify goals and directions for the church in its next 25 years. One task given to congregants in 1980 was to write a story that projected what a fictional "Jack, Jill and child" would find in visiting the church for the first time in 2000.

One person wrote: *"A bus picks up members because of the fuel shortage. . . . The tuition for the Religious Education seems high (remember, it was only $10/year back in 1980) but all the teachers are paid professionals. Volunteers ran out in 1981, with the continued entry of both parents into the working force. . . . There is a full range of Sunday activities for all the family members with the ever-widening acceptance of the four-day work week. Sundays are a family recreation day, centered around the church. Most families conduct their business and related needs on Friday and Saturday, and use Sundays as renewal periods among friends in the church. There are wellness groups, outing clubs (using the buses), extended family gatherings, and youth-centered activities. . . . First Universalist Church is still looking for a janitor!"*

Another wrote: *"The electrically powered mini-cab dropped them off at the door. The cab's computer pilot immediately re-directed it to another address in south Minneapolis where someone had requested transportation. Although it was mid-November, the church building was a comfortable 68 degrees inside. The solar heating system, installed in 1987, was functioning well. . . . The usher had received a briefing from the computer and knew a little about Jack and his family. He knew they were interested in the preschool program, and directed them to the church school area. The teacher was expecting Janie and greeted her by name. . . . Jack and Jill entered the [sanctuary]. The pianist had begun the prelude: a Schubert sonata. Unlike some churches in the area, First Universalist had chosen not to hook into the computerized religious music network—liberal humanist division. They chose instead the tradition of music performed live."*

The Futures Committee formed five teams to gather information about trends in: 1) Unitarian Universalist attitudes, beliefs and values; 2) church membership; 3) church services to members; and 4) the church

Of 12 major areas of concern affecting the future, the Long Range Planning Committee (the renamed Futures Committee) in 1982 identified three to focus efforts on: 1) Conflict resolution, i.e., seeking non-violent solutions to differences; 2) Housing, i.e., examining solutions for seniors, singles, one-parent families and young families; 3) Global education, i.e., supporting efforts to educate through church school, public schools, community forums and media.

A new concern was also raised by some members of the committee. Would the conservative-based Moral Majority "be a force that we are going to have to deal with for the next several years? What kind of profile should we take as a congregation? There is a certain sense of threat because of their political implications. Do we need to be worried about it?"

role in community life in the Twin Cities area. A fifth team was designed for resource support and communication to the congregation.

The Reverend John Cummins delivered several sermons in 1980 about future concerns, including "Our Children's Future." Outside experts were brought in for forums about the implications for the church of trends in architecture, technology, education, politics, energy, communications and more.

One of the trends that emerged during the work, was the request for more feeling, soothing rituals, group singing, "or as we finally defined it, a goose bump [factor] to help balance the equally important but sometimes dry logical and cerebral parts of our services. Many teenage children have definitely noticed this lack and reach out to other religious groups and public organizations to help satisfy their needs." Church members also wanted to become more involved in developing and participating in church services and programs, and a significant number wanted to integrate the children's church experience into that of the larger community.

It was suggested that a Coming of Age curriculum be added. "Many of the children's parents are at First Universalist Church because they have walked away from something else; their children have not walked away from anything. They need a strong sense of our history to understand and embrace our beliefs, especially in these days of the Moral Majority."

Another said, "Our church is supposed to be so much more family oriented than, say, the Unitarian Society. Yet as families enter our church, they immediately split, children to church school, parents to Sunday service." The report indicated, "We take them to the ballet, to the symphony, to the theater, but not to church," and suggested developing an intergenerational committee that could design activities in sports, creative arts, book discussion, ecological issues.

By 2009, First Universalist Church had incorporated many of these forward-thinking ideas into its structure and activities. It remained to be seen how the congregation and church staff would implement its vision for the future. — *Mikki Morrissette*

Our distinctive history, our Universalist heritage, and our hopes for the future inspire us to give generously of our time, our talents and our resources to further our common congregational mission and vision.
—excerpt of the First Universalist Church Vision Statement, adopted by the congregation in 2008

The Reverend Justin Schroeder
Inspire the Future

The Reverend Justin Schroeder was raised as a Unitarian Universalist (UU) in Colorado, where the seeds of his ministry were planted while looking up at the mountains and the Milky Way. He earned a bachelor of arts in English with a creative writing emphasis at Colorado State University and master of divinity at Meadville Lombard Theological School in 2007. He met his wife, Juliana Keen, at a Unitarian Universalist young adult conference in Denton, Maryland. Keen worked at interfaith organizations as a community organizer and program director and received her masters of social work and masters of public policy degrees from the University of Minnesota.

The Reverend Justin Schroeder, his wife Juliana Keen, and their son, Tucker

We seek a minister who delivers intellectually compelling and spiritually inspiring sermons. We seek a leader who can build relationships, both within the church and with the wider world.
—Two priorities from the 2008 Ministerial Search congregational survey and focus group interviews

Schroeder's vision for ministry was shaped and formed by 12 years of experience working in UU congregations. He worked with youth at Foothills Unitarian Church in Colorado, was the Director of Young Adult and Campus Ministry—and later acting assistant minister—at All Souls Unitarian Church in Tulsa, Oklahoma. He relocated to Unity Church-Unitarian in Saint Paul in 2006. In quick succession, he became Unity's co-sabbatical minister, with all the duties of a senior minister, and then director of congregational development.

The Search Committee introduced Schroeder to the congregation with these words: *Justin is energetic and compelling in the pulpit, and his sermons are accessible and profound, authentic and theologically balanced. At the core of Justin's ministry is the idea that, in his words, it matters deeply how we greet, see, and receive each other. Thus whether the topic is new member integration or faith in action, Justin sees community building as foundational to his ministry. The Search Committee is confident that Justin will draw out the best of who we are as a religious community as he challenges us to live up to what our faith calls us to be: radically welcoming, spiritually grounded, and justice seeking."*

I hope for an intergenerational ministry, one that is collaborative and spirit-filled, that is grounded in a clear mission and vision and connects us with our deepest callings. I imagine a ministry that actively helps us grow our souls, serves the world, and is committed to anti-racism, anti-oppression, social justice, and care for the natural environment, as we seek to make real the beloved community.
—the Reverend Justin Schroeder, during the ministerial search process when he was asked to describe the ministry he seeks

Sermons from Candidating Week

I wonder if we might try this answer, when people ask us, "What do Unitarian Universalists believe? There's certainly a lot we could say, including, "Historically, we believe in one God, no one left behind," or "We believe that we don't have to think alike to love alike" or "We're connected more by shared values than shared beliefs"…all of which are fine answers.

But since Unitarian Universalism is, after all, the story, over the centuries, of the stripping away of the religious creeds and dogmas that cripple and constrain the human spirit, I really do think we should try, "We believe in loving God and loving our neighbors as ourselves."

It's a perfectly Unitarian Universalist response! There's no trinity, no "Jesus is the only way," no hell. It points to the heart of what a religious life and a religious community should be about. And it points to the heart of my ministry. The commandment to "Love God and love your neighbor" is not doctrine or creed, but an invitation into deeper faith. It is an invitation to practice and to promise radical love, devotion, hospitality, and generosity in our lives. And the church is the place where we practice and promise this together, in community—*it's what the church is in the world to do.*

—"Practices and Promises," April 26, 2009

Friends, we are surrounded by a mighty cloud of witnesses. The air whispers their names. Our lives, and indeed this very place, is infused with the dreams, hopes, and gifts of those who have gone before us. And the gift that we have been given in this church is the bold and life-changing claim that love and hope are stronger than death and loss, that there are no disposable people, that no one will be left behind, that the embrace of love extends to every single human being.

One hundred and fifty years ago, a small group of brave and hearty souls founded this church, and through the generations, their vision has been kept alive by the faithful who have tended to the fire, and to the embers, when the fire burned low.

Now, it is our turn to add the fuel of our lives to this faith. As we move forward together into a future we can only begin to imagine, may we remember our ancestors, our loved ones, the "great oaks" who have helped bring us to this point. Let us never forget the gifts they have entrusted to us. Let us never forget that we have come into this world . . . to be filled with light, and to shine.

—"When I Am Among the Trees," May 3, 2009

Illuminate the Past, Celebrate the Present, Inspire the Future   145

WE WILL

It's a long path we've set our feet upon

Noted folk singer Ann Reed wrote a song in honor of the 150th anniversary of First Universalist Church of Minneapolis called "We Will" and led the congregation in singing it at our Sesquicentennial Soiree in 2009.

And with loving hearts walk on

We will walk on . . .

Bridges begin with open hands
We begin to heal the world
We will heal the world . . .

*When the sun shines
through all of us*

There on the road

*Will be a rainbow
in front of us*

Wherever we go

Wherever we go

Take a single flame and pass it on

It's enough to light the way

We will light the way . . .

Illuminate the Past, Celebrate the Present, Inspire the Future 149

All the souls who came before are standing here

You can hear them whisper low

We will walk with you

Dreams and Legacies

If all our relations with this Church have tended to make us better men, better women, better youth, then what manner of service should we render in carrying forward the work of our beloved Church? What resolutions should we make that, so far as our efforts can contribute, the next half century shall as far exceed in richness of result that just ended as the field of its activities has grown greater?
—Major William D. Hale, spoken in 1909, at the 50th anniversary celebration

My hope is that the children of our church grow up in a world where the values of inclusion, respect, questioning, love for earth and humanity guide their actions and their thoughts all through their days.
— Heidi Mastrud, First Universalist Church, Director of Congregational Life

Everyone needs a driving dream. In one of mine, war is abolished and First Universalist becomes the best peace site in the world.
— Lynn Elling, member since 1948

Travelers are we all whose eternal journey is toward the future: climbing barriers, crossing mountains, through the gaping centuries we stride out into the unknown, into the unseen, and in our blood the trumpet sounds: "Beyond all borders! Go beyond!"
—the Reverend John Cummins

I envision a beautiful sanctuary where we are proud to hold our services. It is a place where all who enter find joy and comfort . . . one that radiates our spirit and is welcoming to all.
—Bette DeMars, Visual Arts and SPIFF

My hope is for our church to be as influential in the next 150 years as we've been in the first 150. Living our principles and inviting others to join in our vision of justice, service and love.
—Jenny Thomas, Sesquicentennial Committee

Connections with one another matter. Having a powerful transformative Sunday worship experience matters. Those are the building blocks for how we move into the future. When I think about the next 150 years, I am excited about what this church can do when we get all the pieces and parts aligned and are clear about where we are going and how we want to be in the world.
—the Reverend Justin Schroeder

Acknowledgements

The labor of love that you hold in your hands was the product of years of gestation involving an extensive team. The process started when a handful of people held weekly working sessions at the church for six months, sorting out the guts of dozens of disparate boxes dislodged from corners of the First Universalist Church, to create archival boxes of information categorized and organized—in some cases outlined and summarized—so that researchers could access them in the future. The archive team was led and coordinated by Mikki Morrissette. John Addington worked faithfully, rarely missing a week. Carol Jackson single-handedly looked at every image and organized them into topics, handing off hundreds of the strongest images for Jeff Sylvestre and Rod Nordberg to scan. This became an intergenerational venture; even 10-year-old Sophia Morrissette scanned images. Jessica Wicks set about the task of finding some of the juiciest tidbits hidden in the files, and figured out how to organize the images into more easily accessible categories.

Marcia Wattson worked with a committee to develop a skeleton for this book, tapping into the wealth of wisdom in the congregation to find writers and researchers for articles. Many of them appeared in shorter form in *The Liberal* newsletter. The writing team included: John Addington, Betsy Allis, Chris Bremer, Bette DeMars, Judy Goebel, Dave Juncker, Mary Junge, Peg Meier, Marie Nordberg, Paul Riedesel, Dick Saunders, Pamela Vincent, Jessica Wicks, Karin Wille, and others who contributed tendons and joints to make connections with the links of our past.

Then it was time to flesh things out. Morrissette and the archivists dug for missing images and facts. Teams went to the Minnesota History Center to pick through 12 boxes of church archives that the Reverend John Cummins had taken there years earlier. Sylvestre, who was simultaneously creating the Sesquicentennial DVD, took snapshots of images that could not be scanned. Morrissette began to assemble and design the articles, images and individual facts into book form.

Kathy Coskran was tapped to breathe life into the narrative of 150 years of history, by adding heart and soul to the flesh and bones. She reorganized, tweaked and refined while Morrissette continued to check facts, lay out text and add images. Morrissette and Coskran absorbed the comments and suggestions of a book review committee. For several months, Nancy Atchison, Wille, Wattson, Jackson, Nordberg and Junge offered input about how to make improvements to what continued to develop and grow over the Summer of 2009.

Finally, with a due date of October 24, 2009, the team delivered. We know this labor of love is not complete. There will undoubtedly be a few pinched nerves when we discover what was missed, and when some recollections of history are clarified by others. But years of blood, sweat and even a few tears led to the evolution of this 150-years-in-the-making First Universalist Church of Minneapolis book of history.

Enjoy. Share. Talk about it on Cyber Coffeehour. But most of all, admire. There is a tremendous amount of information in these pages that we, as a congregation, can be proud of.

co-editors Mikki Morrissette (top) and Kathy Coskran (below)

SESQUICENTENNIAL STEERING COMMITTEE

Sesquicentennial Steering Committee members: (back row) Jeff Sylvestre, Karin Wille, Pamela Vincent, Peg Meier, Marcia Wattson, Marie Nordberg, (front row) Nancy Atchison, Carol Jackson, Bette DeMars. Not pictured: Mikki Morrissette and Jenny Thomas.

Our dream for the future is that the next 150 years will be as significant in peoples' lives and the community as the first 150 have been. We hope we will continue to thrive in the city of Minneapolis and the denomination. Our ultimate hope is that the work started by the Sesquicentennial Steering Committee will continue: that we will continue to find the volunteers and historians who will maintain, treat precious and give access to our wonderful archives, allowing everyone the opportunity to learn even more about ourselves, to tell anyone and everyone who will listen about how wonderful the First Universalist Church of Minneapolis really is.

APPENDIX

First Universalist Ministers

Joseph Willard Keyes	1863-1866
James Harvey Tuttle	1866-1891
Marion Daniel Shutter, Assistant	1886-1891
Marion Daniel Shutter	1891-1939
Carl Harold Olson	1939-1963
Kenneth Marshall, Assistant	1958-1960
John Cummins	1963-1986
David Phreaner, Assistant	1983-1984
Armida Alexander, Interim	1986-1987
Theodore (Ted) Webb, Interim	1987-1988
Frank Lowell (Terry) Sweetser, Jr. and Mary Susan Milnor, Co-Ministers	1988-1995
Gretchen Thompson, Community Associate Minister	1994-1995
Wayne Robinson, Interim	1995-1996
Sheryl Wurl, Interim	1995-1996
Ken Brown, Interim	1996-1997
Frank Rivas	1997-2007
Charlotte Cowtan, Interim	2007-2009
Kathleen (Kate) Tucker, Associate	1997-
Justin Schroeder	2009-

CONGREGATIONAL PRESIDENTS
FIRST UNIVERSALIST CHURCH OF MINNEAPOLIS

(* incomplete records)

1866 – 1897	Dorilus Morrison
1897 – 1909	William D. Washburn
1909 – 1919*	John Washburn
1919 – 1934*	William G. Northrup
1934 – 1935	Albert Cobb
1935 – 1950	Alfred F. Pillsbury
1950 – 1959*	Rollin Andrews, Lyndon M. King
1959 – 1960	Lynn Elling
1960 – 1963	Don Carter
1963 – 1965	Charles M. Slocum
1965 – 1967	Myrna Hansen
1967 – 1968	David Hersey
1968 – 1970	Warren Gammell
1970 – 1971	Thomas Anderson
1971 – 1973	Douglas Frost
1973 – 1975	Dodd Wilson
1975 – 1977	Mary McGarraugh
1977 – 1979	John Westrom
1979 – 1981	Sharon Bishop
1981 – 1984	Nancy Atchison
1984 – 1986	Carol Jackson
1986 – 1987	Harlan Limpert
1987 – 1988	Drusilla Cummins
1988 – 1990	Karin Wille
1990 – 1992	Bill McKnight
1992 – 1993	Kathy Coskran
1993 – 1994	Marty Sozansky
1994 – 1996	Eugene Link
1996 – 1998	Margit Berg
1998 – 1999	Laura Cooper
1999 – 2001	Ginny McAninch
2001 – 2003	Harlan Limpert
2003 – 2005	David Lauth
2005 – 2006	Marcia Wattson
2006 – 2007	Bill Elwood
2007 – 2009	Sue Schiess
2009 – 2010	Barry Johnson

Appendix

First Universalist Denominational Officials

Universalist Church of America

President
William Drew Washburn

Trustees
The Reverend Marion Shutter
The Reverend Carl Olson

Unitarian Universalist Association

Board of Trustees
Drusilla Cummins
The Reverend Terry Sweetser

Nominating Committee
Nancy Atchison
Helene Haapala

District President's Association
Carol Jackson, President and Treasurer

Annual Program Fund Chair
Nancy Atchison

Regional Subcommittee on Candidacy
Nancy Atchison
Karin Wille

President's Roundtable Local Planning
Bill Elwood
Carol Jackson
Karin Wille

General Assembly Local Arrangements
David Lauth

Prairie Star District

Board of Directors
The Reverend John Cummins, President
Nancy Atchison, President
Carol Jackson, President and Treasurer
Bill Elwood, Treasurer
Drusilla Cummins
Lionel Barker
Rex Gaskill
David Leppik

Ministerial Settlement Representative
The Reverend John Cummins
Sue Schiess

Compensation Consultant
Karin Wille

Carl H. Olson Ministerial Education Fund Recipients

This fund, established in the 1960s and funded by the members at First Universalist, provides stipends for students studying for the Unitarian Universalist ministry and for First Universalist interns.

Armida Alexander

Lee Barker

Leonetta Bugleisi

Laurie Bushbaum

Petr Dolak

Ian S. Evison

Laurel Hallman

Linda Hansen

Linda Hart

Roberta Haskins

Kathryn Hawbaker

Kent Hemmen Seleska

Carol Hepokoski

Wesley Hromatko

Ralph O. Johnson

Robert Karnan

Derek Kiewatt

Harlan Limpert

Peter Luton

Christana Wille McKnight

Lynn Mikula

Charles Ortman

Suzanne Owens-Pike

Meg Riley

Long-Term Members' Anniversaries

listed by date of membership

Donna Elling 11/14/1948
Lynn Elling 11/14/1948
Barbara Whipple 4/18/1954
Kenneth Heidelberg 4/10/1955
Ruth Heidelberg 4/10/1955
Daniel Bishop 5/6/1956
James Lund 2/1/1959
Muriel Avery 5/3/1959
Ellen Hughes 12/6/1959
Milton Hughes 12/6/1959
Rosemary Booth 2/14/1960
Don Wilson 3/6/1960
Robert Benjamin 4/4/1960
Frank Blake 6/5/1960
Dru Cummins 11/3/1963
John Cummins 11/3/1963
Robert Henson 2/2/1964
Nancy Atchison 4/12/1964
Thomas Atchison 4/12/1964
James Chandler 4/12/1964
Janet Chandler 4/12/1964
Adele Hersey 5/3/1964
Carol Anderson 1/10/1965
Bruce Hedlund 4/18/1965
HannahRae Hedlund 4/18/1965
Gwendolyn Mosborg 6/7/1965
Preben Mosborg 6/7/1965
Jeanne Irish 12/11/1966
Frederic Johnson 12/11/1966
Jeanne Johnson 12/11/1966
Caroline Mills 12/11/1966
Dennis Mills 12/11/1966
Jerry Raich 2/20/1968
Carol Flynn 4/30/1968
Mary Djerf 10/22/1968
Karen Ziegler 10/22/1968
Richard Ziegler 10/22/1968
Gail Hanson 11/19/1968

Stuart Hanson 11/19/1968
Sylvia Rudolph 3/21/1971
Donald Ryberg 11/16/1971
Dale Schwie 12/14/1971
Kay Schwie 12/14/1971
Raymond Warner Jr. 8/15/1972
Susan Bidwell 3/22/1973
Pauline Schuller 5/15/1973
Marian Kosobayashi 9/18/1973
William Lancaster 10/16/1973
Riley M. Owens 10/16/1973
Larry Gottschalk 11/20/1973
David Juncker 11/20/1973
Gertrude Juncker 11/20/1973
Pat Gottschalk 12/18/1973
Arlene Jacobson 12/18/1973
Harlan Limpert 4/30/1974
Robert Moe 11/19/1974
Mae Warner 11/19/1974
Kay Hawbaker 9/23/1975
Dick Niemiec 9/23/1975
Joan Niemiec 9/23/1975
Alfred Harrison 4/20/1976
Ingrid Harrison 4/20/1976
Amy Engberg 1/18/1977
John Engberg 1/18/1977
Carol Jackson 4/19/1977
Carolyn Moe 9/20/1977
Margit Berg 10/18/1977
Thomas Berg 10/18/1977
Karin Wille 12/20/1977
Chris Bremer 10/17/1978
Raleigh Little 10/17/1978
Jack Shelton 10/17/1978
Dave Arnold 1/16/1979
Ruth Arnold 1/16/1979
Joyce Riedesel 1/16/1979
Paul Riedesel 1/16/1979
Charles Coskran 2/20/1979

Kathleen Coskran 2/20/1979
Mary DeBruin 2/20/1979
Robert DeBruin 2/20/1979
Jan Wagener 3/20/1979
Pat Wagener 3/20/1979
Susan Jones 11/20/1979
Mary Loberg 1/15/1980
Eileen Nelson 2/19/1980
Lewis Bishop 3/18/1980
Daniel McLaughlin 3/18/1980
Sharon McLaughlin 3/18/1980
Marjie Smith 6/17/1980
Marjorie Herdes 10/21/1980
Jerry Machalek 12/16/1980
Meredith Smith 1/20/1981
Julie Howard 2/17/1981
William Howard 2/17/1981
Ann Hobbs 3/17/1981
Howard Hobbs 3/17/1981
Karen Bruce 10/20/1981
Karen Chandler 10/20/1981
David Showalter 1/19/1982
Susan Showalter 1/19/1982
Marcia Wattson 2/16/1982
Jane Hallas 4/20/1982
Janet Mills 3/15/1983
Kathleen Olson 3/15/1983
John Addington 4/3/1983
Bette DeMars 4/19/1983
John DeMars 4/19/1983
James Block 11/17/1983
Rene Block 11/17/1983
William Kirkpatrick 11/17/1983
Betsy Long 2/16/1984
Virginia McAninch 3/15/1984
Philip Johnson 4/19/1984
Mary Weeks 4/19/1984
Carol Johnson 10/18/1984

SURNAMES OF OUR FOUNDING MEMBERS

based on recollections at the 50th anniversary celebration in 1909

At Cataract House, 1859

Chowen
Cornell
Eastman
Gibson
King
Morrison
Pray
Washburn
Whitmore

By 1874

Aldrich
Babbs
Barton
Baxter
Beal
Birge
Bowsman
Brackett
Brigham
Burr
Cadwell
Cahill
Carpenter
Case
Chase
Conkey
Cooper
Couchman
Coykendall
Cuings
Day
Dillingham
Eldridge
Elliot
Eustis
Farnham
Gardner
Gilson
Gold
Goodwin
Greenleaf
Hale
Hawkins
Herrick
Holmes
Hunter
Koon
Lamborn
Loring
Lowry
Marchant
Marshall
Mattison
McMillan
Morgan
Mulford
Northrup
Pierce
Plumer
Provan
Rand
Roberts
Robinson
Russell
Sayer
Shepley
Shuler
Stanchfield
Stevens
Stickney
Sweet
Taylor
Thompson
Veazies
Wiggins
Wilcox
Woodward

Harrison Salisbury

In 1919, Harrison Salisbury, the 11-year-old son of Mr. and Mrs. Percy Pritchard Salisbury, 109 Royalston Avenue North, was baptized at Church of the Redeemer. Salisbury was the future Pulitzer Prize-winning journalist who served as The New York Times bureau chief in Moscow and was the first editor of the Times' Op-Ed page. Salisbury's 9-year-old sister Janet was baptized the same day.

1885 Sunday School

A class at Church of the Redeemer, taught by W. P. Roberts, with Mrs. Evelyn Burt as singing director, consisted of these high school-aged girls:

Onata Kerr, Lena Stickney, Effie Ames, Esther Friedlander, Mabel Gordon, Maude Edwards, Mamie Lowry, Mary Washburn, Lulu Camp, Tillie Filbert, Gertrude Fox, Nellie Hale, F. Gartney Lawrence, Irene Robinson, Stella Winston, Jeannette Brewer, Maude Shannon, Greta Kisser, Edna Cooper

First Universalist Church
2008 Vision Statement

adopted by the Congregation, March 9, 2008

First Universalist Church of Minneapolis, founded in 1859, is a large, dynamic religious community where congregants, including members and friends of all ages, draw spiritual inspiration from the principles of Unitarian Universalism to work together to make our world a better place.

Congregants of all ages joyously learn and work together to understand and live the values and principles of our faith. Children and youth are guided and mentored by spiritually grounded adults.

We seek lifelong spiritual growth. Individually, with others, and in community, we participate in religious education, spiritual practice and self-reflection. We join in inspirational worship that interweaves the intellect, the spirit and the arts to create an experience of the sacred, including rituals of blessing and celebration.

We warmly welcome newcomers into our community. We are enriched by the diverse identities and perspectives of all who join their personal spiritual journeys with our common vision. We offer meaningful opportunities for participation to all and invite deep interpersonal connections. We care for one another in times of need.

Our ministers' and congregants' prophetic voices inspire courageous transformational actions to further peace, justice, and environmental stewardship. As leaders and participants, we join in this work and in service to others with other Unitarian Universalists, with those of other faiths, and with secular organizations.

Our distinctive history, our Universalist heritage, and our hopes for the future inspire us to give generously of our time, our talents and our resources to further our common congregational mission and vision.

We are a well-governed congregation whose democratically empowered leaders earn the trust of members by being responsible stewards of our facility and our human and financial resources so that we may, together, realize the congregation's vision for today, and for times we shall never see.

SESQUICENTENNIAL STEERING COMMITTEE

CHAIRS AND DONORS

Steering Committee Co-Chairs
Nancy Atchison and Karin Wille

Honorary Chair
The Reverend John Cummins, Minister Emeritus

Honorary Fundraising Co-Chairs
Kim Lund
Mark Ritchie

Sesquicentennial Donors

Bob Albrecht
Carol & Tom Anderson
Dave & Ruth Arnold
Tom & Nancy Atchison,
Bob Benjamin & Cathy Coult
Dan Berg & Welcome Jerde
Tom & Margit Berg
David Caccamo & Sofia Ali
Elsa Carpenter
Laura & Ben Cooper
Chuck & Kathy Coskran
Charlotte Cowtan
John & Dru Cummins
John & Bette DeMars
Mary Djerf & Don Wilson
George Dow & Bonnie Hill
Lynn & Donna Elling
Nancy Gaschott & Mark Ritchie
Judy & Ray Goebel

Bill & Julie Howard
Barry & Karen Johnson
Jane & Joel Johnson
Philip & Mary Weeks Johnson
Richard Kain
Ann Kay
Barbara Kellett
Bill Kirkpatrick & Susan Bidwell
David Lauth & Lindsey Thomas
Geoff Lenox & Anne McBean
Harlan Limpert
Kim Lund
Mary Mahoney & Dennis Dischinger
Ginny McAninch
Preston & Betsy McMillan
Peg Meier & Rebecca Lindholm
Joan & Rick Naymark

Dick & Joan Niemiec
David Potyondy & Lianne Knych
Lyn Rabinovitch & John Saxhaug
Paul & Joyce Riedesel
Tom Rush & Nora Whiteman
Sherry & Tom Saterstrom
Sue & Gary Schiess
John & Rebecca Shockley
Lisa Sinclair
Lynne Stanley & Chris Elliott
Kim & Caren Stelson
Jennifer & David Thomas
Kate Tucker
Pamela Vincent
Marcia Wattson
Karin Wille
Paige Winebarger
Karen & Richard Ziegler

INDEX

100 Years of Liberation AUW, Minneapolis, 22, 52, 79, 115-116
50th Anniversary, x, 6, 13-14, 21, 29, 64-65, 79-80, 110, 135
100th Anniversary, 137-138
150th Anniversary, 138, 139-140

A

About Your Sexuality (AYS), 76
Addington, Fran, ii, 84; line drawings vi, viii, ix, 2
Addington, John, ii, iv, x, 14, 31, 38, 44, 46, 59, 96, 120, 131, 151
AIDS, 118-120
Alexander, Armida, 49, 153, 156
Aliveness Project, The, 124, 125
All-Church Council, 87, 111
Allis, Betsy, 115, 124, 129-130, 151
Ames, Effie, 77
Anderson, Curt, 79-80
Anderson, Thomas, 154
Andrews, Mary Garard, 22, 114
Andrews, Rollin, 22, 35, 154
Anthony, Susan B., 12
Arnold, Ruth, 82, 111
Arnold, Steve, 82
Articles of Incorporation, 66-68, 85
Association of Universalist Women (AUW), xi, 4, 21, 22, 50, 52, 73, 75, 79, 84, 96, 113-117, 131
Atchison, Nancy, ii, 36, 55, 130, 140, 151, 152, 154, 155, 160
Atchison, Tom, 55, 126, 131
Athenaeum, 4, 18
Avidor, Roberta, ii

B

Bailey, Christine, 84
Baldwin, David, 83
Ballou, Robert O., 75
Barber-Braun, Sarah, 19
Barker, Lee, 78, 140, 155
Barker, Lionel, 78, 155

Barker, Beverly, 77, 78
Barnes, Mikesha, 123
Barnes, Seth, 11
Barton, Clara, 16, 113-114
Befrienders, 44, 112
benediction, 42, 70, 100, 108, 137
Benjamin, Bette, 114, 116
Berg, Dan, 124
Berg, Julia, 124
Berg, Margit, 111, 154
Berg, Tom, 36
Bible, 15, 65-67, 75, 89, 91-93, 96, 127, 137
Bielke, Marge, 51
Bisbee, Herman, 31, 89, 92-93
Bishop, Dan, 60, 84
Bishop, Frederica, 115
Bishop, Lewis, 36
Bishop, Sharon, 71-72, 84, 114-115, 118-119, 129, 131, 154
Blackmer Home for Women, 117
Blanchard, June, 60
Blum, Christina, 83
Board of Trustees, First Universalist, 4-6, 18, 22, 35, 42, 52, 69, 80, 85, 88, 112-113, 115-116, 118, 136
Board of Trustees, Unitarian Universalist Association, 54
Bohman, Mary, 81
Bond of Fellowship, 65-68
Bonn, Jim, 80
Boston Declaration, 65-68
Brackett, George A., 5, 6
Bremer, Chris, 16, 26, 151
Bretz, Gertrude, 24
Broad, Judy, 124
Brown, Harvey, 6
Brown, Ken, 44, 46, 49, 120, 153
Bruce, Karen, 118
Buckley, Jean, 124
Buddha, 97, 98
Buddhism, 45, 105
Building and Grounds (BAG), 60, 128
Burk, Claire, 50, 51

Burke, Phil, x
Burt, Evelyn, 77
Bushbaum, Laurie, 72, 77-78, 84, 115, 155
Bushnell, Horace, 11

C
Capek, Norbert, 70
Carbine, Pat, 114
Carl Olson Ministerial Education Fund, 52
    Carl Olson fund recipients, 156
Carlson, Arnie, 115
Carlson, Nancy, 76, 78
Carpenter, Gracie, 84
Carter, Don, 60, 154
Carter, Mary E., 60
Casserly, Mike, ii
Cataract House, vi, 2, 28, 85
Catholic Archdiocese, vii, 31, 34, 37, 56
Central American Human Rights 127
Chandler, Janet, 57, 80-81
Chandler, Jim, 57
child dedications, xi, 70
children, 5-6, 12, 19, 24-26, 38, 44, 51, 57, 69, 70, 108, 113, 124, 132, 137, 142
Chowen, George, 85
Christian, 12, 52, 67, 70, 76, 89, 92, 94, 112, 138
Christianity, xi, 12-13, 62, 64, 75, 91
Christianson, Milo, 25
Christmas, 82, 84, 107, 113
church buildings
   3400 Dupont Avenue South, ix, 44, 57-59, 60, 82-84, 101, 123
   4600 Dupont Avenue South, viii, 33-34, 38, 56, 61, 83
   5000 Girard Avenue South, viii, 33-34, 38, 43-44, 56-58, 60, 66, 69, 79, 83, 89, 111, 132, 137
   Fifth Street and Fourth Avenue, ii, vi, 13, 28
   Eighth Street and Second Avenue, vii, 1, 13, 28-31, 34
Church of the Redeemer, vii, xi, 1-2, 6, 11, 15, 20, 22, 23, 25-26, 28- 31, 32, 37-38, 50, 56, 64, 70, 77, 82, 85, 90, 93, 108, 113, 110, 117, 121, 132, 135-136, 158
civil rights, 41, 98, 113, 126
Cobb, Albert, 154
Coming of Age (COA), 73, 77, 108, 142
Communism, 41, 94, 138
congregational presidents, 154
Confucius, 97
congregational polity, 69, 85
Constitution, First Universalist Society, 64-66, 86
Cooper, Barclay, 11, 20
Cooper, Laura, 45, 154
Cooperstein, Eric, 122
Cornell, F. R. E., 85
Cornell, George, 3, 32
Cornell, William, 85
Coskran, Kathy, ii, 36, 44, 45, 55, 73, 98, 100, 104, 106, 151, 154
Cowtan, Charlotte, 49, 153
Crane, Peter, 84
Crocker, George D., 3, 32, 85
Crocker, George, 127
Crosby, Caroline M., 19, 22, 25-26
Crosby, John, 6, 17, 19
Cummins Room, 59, 83
Cummins, Drusilla, 40-41, 55, 83, 109, 114, 154, 155
Cummins, John, viii, 35, 40-41, 42, 49, 50-51, 52, 55, 60, 62, 67-68, 70, 75, 83, 85-86, 89, 98-99, 100, 111, 114, 118, 126, 127, 132, 133, 139, 142, 150, 151, 153, 160
Cummins, Robert, 37-38, 40, 96, 98, 139
Currie, Constance and Edward, 25
Cyber Coffeehour, 36, 120

D
Dahmes, Shannon, 108
Darwin, Charles, vi, 31, 84, 92-93
Dean, Mary Ann, 51
DeMars, Bette, 83-84, 150, 152
DeMars, John, 118

denominational officials, First Universalist, list of, 155
Djerf, Mary, 51
Douglass, Frederick, 12
Dreessen, Viola K., 78
Dubois, Paul Martin, 130

E
Earth Day, 128
Eastman Fund, 111
Eastman, William, 21
EcoMinds 128
Edie, Jack, 132
Eginton, Lael, 82
Elling, Donna, 132
Elling, Lynn, 39, 132, 138, 154
Eliot, Frederick May, 102
Ellison, Keith, 130
Elwood, Bill, 154, 155
Emerson, Ralph Waldo, 92
environmental programs, 128-129, 131
Equal Rights Amendment, (ERA), 113-114
Ernst, Grace, 79
Esch, Tom, 130
Evershed, Jane, 84
evolution, xi, 15-16, 89, 92-94, 139

F
Fahs, Sophia, 75-76, 137-138
Felman, Lynn, 84
Field and the Fruit, The, 13, 90, 135
fire department, 2, 5
First Universalist Society of St. Anthony, 11, 31, 92
First Universalist Foundation, xi, 26, 36, 116, 121-122, 124
First Universalist Society, vi, xi, 2, 4-5, 7, 9, 13, 17-18, 64-65, 82, 86, 92, 108
flower communion, 69-71
Fonda, Henry, 25
font, baptismal, 32, 57
founders, First Universalist Society, 3-4, 17, 34, 62, 64,

founding members, surnames, 158
Friedlander, Esther, 4
Frost, Douglas, 154
Futures Committee, 141-142

G
Galazen, A. J., 120
Gammell, Warren, 154
Garland, W. D., 85
Gay, Lesbian, Bisexual, Transgender (GLBT), 44, 119-120, 131
Gandhi, 98
Gaskill, Rex, 155
General Assembly, 54-55, 67, 114
General Mills, xi, 18-19
Gibson, Paris, 6, 14
Giles, Philip, 137
God, xi, 20, 38, 47, 62-68, 70, 77, 91-95, 97, 99, 102, 104-105, 106-107, 127, 137, 144
Goebel, Judy, 88, 151
Goff, Shari, 78
Graham, Arthur, 42, 100
Graham, Billy, 96, 138
Great Depression, 37, 94
Green, Richard, 132
Griffith, Marion, 31-32, 38, 50

H
Haberman, Jo, 129-130
Hamilton, Lois, 129
Hale, William D., 29, 64, 79-80, 136, 150
Hansen, Myna, 35, 113, 154
Hapala, Helene, 155
Harriet Tubman Women's Shelter, 124
Harris, Verna, 39
Harvard Divinity School, 40, 42, 43
Harvard University, 15
Hastings, Emil, 78, 83
Hastings, Lillian, 78
Harrison Hall, 28
Hart, Jim, 80
Hate Free Zone, 120
Hayes, Curtiss, 39

Heaton, Katie, 78
Heinrich, Lisa, 60
Her, Kia, 123
Hersey, David, 154
Hicks, Doug, 83
History of the City of Minneapolis, 18, 29
Hobbs, Marabeth, 76
Hobart, Carol, 118
Horizon's Youth Center, 125
Hossly, Elsie, 25
Howard, Frances, 55
Howard, Julie, 111
Howe, Charles A., 66, 68
Hoy, Heidi, 83
Hughes, Evelyn, 50
Hunton, Janice, 81
Hurley, John, 139

I
installation, 38, 42, 69, 74
Interweave, 120, 131

J
Jackson, Carol, 43, 55, 81, 108, 151, 152, 154, 155
Jackson, Tom, ii
Jacobson, Arlene, 111
Japan, 117, 132
Jensen, John, 81, 140
Jerde, Welcome, 124
Jerome, Wendy, 120
Jesus, 62-66, 68, 75, 86, 93-95, 97, 98, 102, 144
Johnson, Barry, 154
Johnson, Carol, 36
Jones-Harrison Home, 6
Jordan, Charles M., 6
Juncker, David, 6, 151
Junge, Mary, ii, x, 8, 51, 77, 112, 116, 151

K
Keen, Juliana, 143
Kellett, Barbara, 55, 73
Ketchum, Kit, 119

Keyes, Reverend Joseph, vi, 10-12, 17, 90, 153
King, John, 39
King, Lyndon, M, 154
King, Dr. Martin Luther, Jr., xi, 35, 41, 98, 109
King, William S., 5, 7, 17
King, W. W., 11
Knuth, Bob, 44, 123, 130
Koon, Martin B., 136
Kung, Hans, 102

L
Labyrinth, 59, 72-73
Ladies' Social Circle, 21, 52, 111
Lakewood Cemetery & Chapel, xi, 2, 7-8, 17, 131
Lamb, Charles, 8
Lappe, Frances Moore, 130
Larger Faith, The, 65, 68
Lauth, David, 132, 154, 155
Leavitt-Phibbs, Dylan, 123
Leppik, David, 155
Liberal, The, x, 36, 50-51, 118, 151
Lifespan Faith Development, 76
Limpert, Harlan, 54, 74, 83, 154, 155
Lincoln, Abraham, 109
Link, Gene, 122, 154
Livingston, David, 81
Loring, Charles M., 4-6, 7, 13, 136
love, xi, 8, 14, 44, 47, 54, 62-68, 89, 91, 95-97, 101-102, 105-108, 111, 134, 136, 144, 151
Lovejoy, Louise Morgan, 29, 136
Lowry, Thomas, 6, 7, 9, 17-18, 30
Luke, Ginger, 43, 55, 78
Lund, Kim, 160
Luton, Peter, 87, 155

M
Machado, Marlon, 127
Maciej, Sharon, 51
Marsh, Charles, 79
Martignacco, Carol, 124
Marshall, Kenneth, 138, 153
Masterson, Earl, 83

Mastrud, Heidi, 78, 150
Matsu San, Koyama, 25
McAninch, Ginny, 154
McClure, Nell, 111
McGarraugh, Mary 154
McKnight, Bill, 154
Mead, Margaret, 110
Meadville-Lombard Theological School, 22, 78, 140, 143
Meier, Peg, x, 6, 151, 152
members' anniversaries, long-term, 157
members, founding 158
Menchu, Rigoberto, 126
Meyer, Helen, 36
Mills, Janet, ii
Milnor, Susan, viii, ix, 42-45, 49, 52, 66, 72, 74, 89, 100-101, 111, 119, 127-128, 130, 153
Minneapolis Institute of Arts, 17-19, 59
Minneapolis Public Library, xi, 4
ministers, First Universalist, list of, 153
Minneapolis Star Journal, 16
Minneapolis Star Tribune, 98, 127
Minneapolis Symphony Orchestra, 9, 79
Minneapolis Tribune, 14, 17, 40, 93
Minnesota UU Social Justice Alliance (MUUSJA), 115, 128-129
Minnesota Valley Unitarian Universalist Fellowship, 49, 55
Moe, Carolyn and Bob, 111
Moral Majority, 141-142
Mooney, Dorothy, 111
Morrill, Ada, 117
Morrison, Clinton, 17-18, 30
Morrison, Dorilus, 4-5, 7, 17-18, 29, 85, 136, 154
Morrissette, Mikki, ii, x, 19, 31, 32, 59, 93, 136, 138, 142, 151, 152
Morrissette, Sophie, 151
Mosborg, Preben, 108
Ms. magazine, 114
Munts, Polly, see Talen, Poly
Murray, John, 63, 65
music, 9, 57, 79-81, 141

music directors, 79-81

N
Ness, Cassi, 111
Neustrom, Luella, 78
Newcomer, Kelly, ii
Niemic, Joan, 36
Nobel Peace Prize Festival, 132
Nordberg, Marie, 41, 48, 81, 151, 152
Nordberg, Rod, 151
Northrup, William G., 154

O
Oberhoffer, Emil J., 9, 79
Olson, Carl, vii, viii, 16, 21, 29, 33, 34, 35, 37-39, 40, 50, 52, 56, 70, 75, 89, 96-97, 111, 126, 137, 153, 155
Olson, Karen, 83
Olson, Mildred Boone, 21, 37, 52, 56
On the Origin of Species, iv, 92
organ, vi, 18, 28, 30, 39, 79-80, 82
Oswood, Bob, 60
Our Lady of Lourdes Catholic Church, 30-31, 130
Our Whole Lives (OWL), 76,
Owens-Pike, Doug, 84

P
Palm, Inger, 60
parks, iv, 2, 5, 17, 19
pastoral care, 47, 49, 51, 106, 111-112
Pathways to Peace, 126
Peace pole, 132
Perkins, Quiana, 124
Perkins, Thomas H., 3, 85
Phreaner, David, 153
Pillsbury, Alfred, 19, 56, 153
Pillsbury, Eleanor, 19
Plumer, H. J., 3, 85
Prairie Star District (PSD), 41, 55, 73, 92, 115, 135
Prayer, 99

Presidents, congregational, (see congregational presidents)
principles, Unitarian Universalist, 61, 62, 65-68, 77
principles, Universalist, 61, 65
Prestemon, Evelyn, 60
Program Council, 87
Prophetic Imperative, The, 130
Pugh, Robert, 35

Q
Quakers, 138

R
Rainbow Families, 120
Rainbow Path, 77
Ramirez, Sharon, ii
Ransom, Anne and Hal, 83
Rasor, Paul, 139
Rausch, Verna, 75
Reagan, Eileen, 81
Reeb, James, 41
Reed, Ann, 140, 145
Reed, D. M., 11
Reilly, Jim, 80-81
Religious Education, 43, 50, 69, 73, 75-78, 87, 137, 139, 141
Religious Education directors, 78
Reyes, Tianna, 125
Riedesel, Paul, 9, 69, 151
Riley, Meg, 54-55, 78, 155
Ritchie, Mark, 36, 109, 131, 160
rituals, 36, 69-70, 72, 74, 107, 142
Rivas, Frank, ix, 45-49, 73, 89, 104-105, 153
Roberts, William P., 21, 77, 108, 136
Robinson, Wayne, 43, 44, 49, 153
Rodgers, Debra, 124
Ryberg, Don and Helen, 132

S
sanctuary movement, 98, 127
Sandburg, Carl, 16
Saunders, Dick, 127, 130, 151
Saunders, Marie, 127
Schiess, Sue, 88, 111-112, 154, 155
Schroeder, Justin, ix, 36, 134, 143-144, 150, 153
Schroeder, Tucker, 143
Schuster-Jaeger, Jennifer, 124
Schwie, Dale, ii
Scofield, E. H. and Mrs., 32, 113
Scofield Wilson, Grace, *See Wilson, Grace*
Scott, Clinton Lee, 105
sesquicentennial, ii, iii, x, xi, 2, 83-84, 134, 139-140, 145, 150, 151, 152
sesquicentennial steering committee, 152
sesquicentennial donors, 160
Sharing Circles, 48, 106
Shutter, Marion, vii, x, 6, 12-14, 15-16, 17, 20, 21, 23, 25, 29-31, 32, 34, 37, 39, 50, 82, 89, 93, 94-95, 96, 110, 117, 135-136, 139, 153, 155
Shutter, Mary (Wilkinson), 6, 15-16, 21, 25
Sibley, Mulford Q., 41
Simpson Transitional Housing, 124
Singing the Living Tradition, 81, 82
Sinkford, Bill, 46
Skinner, Clarence, 65
Skinner, Dolphus, 11
Slocum, Charles M., 154
Snyder, Leslie, 39
Social Justice, 13, 44, 46, 65, 101, 115, 121-124, 126-131
Solstice, 72-73, 115
Sommers, Beverly, 76
Sozansky, Marty, 154
Space, Planning, Improvement, Facilities, and Furnishings (SPIFF) 83, 150
St. Anthony, 3-5, 17, 31, 92-93
Staring, M. S., 11, 21, 93
Steinem, Gloria, 114
Stelson, Aaron, 125
Stelson, Beth, 125
Stockwell, Maud Conkey, 5
Straight, Bilinda, 78
Strong, Elizabeth, 68, 139
Sullivan, Katie, 55

Appendix

Sweetser, Terry, viii, ix, 42-45, 49, 52, 62, 89, 100, 102, 111, 119, 123, 127-128, 130, 153, 155
Sweetser, Henry Chapin, 102
Sylvestre, Jeff, 151, 152

T
Talen, Deborah, 119
Talen, Polly (Munts), 119
theology, 15, 22, 47, 63-65, 69, 75, 77, 89, 94, 100, 105, 106
Thiele, Chuck, 60
Thiele, Gail, 118
This Strange and Wondrous Journey, 41, 99
Thomas, Jenny, 150, 152
Thompson, Gretchen, 74, 103, 130, 153
Tollefson, Ted, 120
TRUST, 47, 112
Tucker, Kate, ix, 45-46, 47-48, 73, 79, 89, 106-107, 112, 140, 153
Tuttle Church, 14, 32, 52, 113
Tuttle, Harriet Merriman, 3, 12, 14, 21
Tuttle, James Harvey, vi, vii, 1, 3, 7, 10, 11, 12-14, 15, 17, 29, 31, 52, 57, 82, 89, 90-94, 113, 135-136, 153

U
Unitarian Universalism, 49, 55, 74, 83, 122, 139, 144
Unitarian Universalist Association (UUA), 41, 46, 54, 61, 66-68, 71, 81, 87, 98, 114, 119, 138
Unitarian Universalist Women's Federation (UUWF), 114-115
Unitarian Universalist(s), 2, 54, 62, 78, 89, 99, 108, 143-144
Unity-Church Unitarian, 120, 143
Unity House, xi, 2, 6, 15, 17, 19, 21, 22, 23-27, 50, 83, 103, 109, 113, 117, 121, 123, 126
Unity Leadership Institute, 122, 123-125,
Unity Settlement Association, 121-122
Unity Summer, xi, 44, 73, 77, 110, 121-125, 130-131

Universalism, 12, 22, 63, 65-66, 68, 92-93, 96, 102, 113, 139,
Universalist Church of America, 37-38, 40, 54-55, 65, 96, 137, 138, 149, 155
University of Minnesota, 4, 19, 24-25, 38, 41, 47, 126, 143
Unitarian Universalist Association (UUA), 41, 46, 49, 54-55, 66-68, 81, 98, 114, 119, 138, 155
Unitarian Universalist Women's Federation (UUWF), 114-116
UU World, 49, 137, 139

V
Vang, Khang, 83
Veatch Foundation, 123, 130
Vietnam War, 35, 98, 126, 130, 140
Vincent, Pamela, 73, 151, 152
Vision Statement, 142, 159
Visual Arts Comitee, 82-84, 150

W
Wackett, Adrian, 108
Wagner, Velma, 119
Walker, Brooks, 49
Walker Methodist Health Center, 125
Washburn Memorial Orphan Home, 5-6, 17
Washburn, Abby, 55
Washburn, Cadwallader, 5, 18
Washburn, Israel, 18
Washburn, John, 154
Washburn, William Drew, 3-6, 7-8, 17, 18, 29, 30, 49, 55, 80, 85, 108, 136, 154, 155
Wattson, Marcia, x, 124, 151, 152, 154
Webb, Ted, 49, 153
Welcome Here Cookbook, 103
Welcome Home Wednesday, 48, 106
Welcoming Congregation, 118-120, 131
Wellstone, Paul, 128
Weston, John, 49
Westrom, John, 154
We Will, 140, 145-149
Whipple, Barbara, 79-80
Whitman, Nora, 108

White, George, 25
Wiesel, Elie, 131
Wicks, Jessica, ii, 90, 94, 117, 120, 151
Wilkins, Craig, x
Wille, Karin, ii, xi, 36, 61, 68, 140, 151, 152, 154, 155, 160
Wilson, Dodd, 154
Wilson, Don, 51
Wilson, Grace Scofield, 52-53, 111, 113
Wilson, Harold, 52
Winchester Profession, 63-68
Women's Association, xi, 19, 21-22, 52, 117
Women's Ritual Circle, 71-72
Woodman Hall, 11, 28
World Citizen, 36, 126, 132
World War II, viii. 35, 39, 117, 126, 132
Worship Associates, 46, 49
Wurl, Sheryl, 44, 49, 120, 130, 153
Wyman, Ralph, 129

Y
youth, 24, 36, 44, 55, 57, 77, 143
Youth Cultural Exchange, xi, 36, 77